KU-495-754

Theory of the Capitalist Economy

Theory of the Capitalist Economy

Towards a post-classical synthesis

Bill Gerrard

Basil Blackwell

Copyright © Bill Gerrard 1989

First published 1989

Basil Blackwell Ltd
108 Cowley Road, Oxford, OX4 1JF, UK

Basil Blackwell Inc.
432 Park Avenue South, Suite 1503
New York, NY 10016, USA

All rights reserved. Except for the quotation of short passages for the purposes of criticism and review, no part of this publication may be reproduced, stored in a retrieval system, or transmitted, in any form or by any means, electronic, mechanical, photocopying, recording or otherwise, without the prior permission of the publisher.

Except in the United States of America, this book is sold subject to the condition that it shall not, by way of trade or otherwise, be lent, re-sold, hired out, or otherwise circulated without the publisher's prior consent in any form of binding or cover other than that in which it is published and without a similar condition including this condition being imposed on the subsequent purchaser.

British Library Cataloguing in Publication Data

Gerrard, Bill
   Theory of the capitalist economy: towards a post-classical synthesis.
   1. Capitalism. Theories
   I. Title
   330. 12′2
   ISBN 0–631–16241–0

Library of Congress Cataloging in Publication Data

Gerrard, Bill.
   Theory of the capitalist economy: towards a post-classical
synthesis / Bill Gerrard.
     p.   cm.
   Bibliography: p.
   Includes index.
   ISBN 0–631–16241–0
   1. Capitalism.   I. Title.
   HB501.G424   1989
   330.12′2—dc19   88–31895
                                                        CIP

Typeset in 11 on 13 pt Times
Printed and bound in Great Britain at
The Camelot Press Ltd, Southampton

For
Norman Dixon, MA, Ph.D., FEIS
Rector of Inverurie Academy 1948–76

From pupil to teacher
in respect and gratitude

The Master said, Yu, shall I teach you
what knowledge is? When you know a thing,
to recognise that you know it, and when
you do not know a thing, to recognise that
you do not know it. That is knowledge.

Confucius, *Analects*

Letting a hundred flowers bloom and a
hundred schools of thought contend is
the policy.

Mao Tse-Tung, *Selected Works*

Contents

Acknowledgements

This is a short book but one with a lengthy history. It represents an attempt to come to terms with the nature of economics. This process began in my undergraduate days at the University of Aberdeen, was fostered in very different ways by my post-graduate studies at Cambridge and the time spent thereafter working as an industrial economist, and has taken shape finally in the last four years in the School of Economic Studies at the University of Leeds. A number of people have given inspiration and invaluable guidance. David Pearce, Bob Elliott and Dave Newlands at Aberdeen; Geoff Harcourt, Bob Rowthorn and Gay Meeks at Cambridge; David Stout at Unilever, and John Hillard and George Rainnie at Leeds all deserve special mention. To them and others, much thanks are due. They supplied most of the pieces of the map, although they may not agree with the way in which they are fitted together, nor may they accept the temporary destination reached.

As regards the manuscript itself, I am very grateful to John Brothwell, Mike Collins, Rodney Crossley, Scott Dickinson, John Goddard, John Hillard and George Rainnie. They read the first draft of the book and gave much constructive criticism and advice. I am particularly grateful to John Hillard, my co-conspirator. We are on the same wavelength but sufficiently out of phase to produce creative interference. I have received invaluable editorial assistance from Mark Allin at Basil Blackwell. His encouragement has been much appreciated. I also wish to thank the two anonymous referees who gave their support to my original proposal for this book. Finally, I must thank Keith Cowling, who, quite anonymously at the time, provided much in the way of helpful and morale-boosting comment on the original proposal and the draft manuscript. Of course, I take full responsibility for the final outcome.

Two groups of people deserve a very heartfelt thanks. First, I must thank the students at Leeds in the classes of 1984–7 and 1985–8, particularly those students who took my final-year optional courses. They were at the sharp end of the development of my ideas, always hearing about 'the book' without actually seeing it. Teaching them did much to clarify matters in my own mind. Second, I must acknowledge the efforts of the secretarial staff, particularly Elsie Merrick, who typed up the early parts of the manuscript, as well as Sue Logan and Pat McDermott, who came to my assistance whenever the word processor was incapable of dealing with my undoubtedly incomprehensible demands.

Last, but by no means least, I must thank my family for their support and encouragement, most particularly Jackie, who had to put up with me during the lows as well as the highs. She was always there to put things in perspective. She got me through.

Preface

It is better to be vaguely right than precisely wrong.

Professor Wildon Carr

This book is motivated by a strong dissatisfaction with the state of modern economic theory. It is a dissatisfaction which began with my first introduction to the subject as an undergraduate. The theoretical models which were presented in the classroom seemed to be based on patently unrealistic assumptions. This scepticism helped insulate me from being totally immersed in the orthodox approach in which I was being educated. I was able to play the theoretical games well, to use the orthodox language, but I never accepted what I was taught.

My scepticism was reinforced by the failure of orthodox economic theory to explain and resolve the problem of mass unemployment. I had turned to economics as a field of study which I, naïvely perhaps, expected to be socially useful. Instead, I found a subject that offered little in the way of hope and constructive policy prescription for solving the greatest economic problem of our time; it seemed truly a dismal science. Fifty years on from the last period of mass unemployment in the Western world, the same economic analysis of unemployment is provided, albeit in a much more sophisticated form, and the same policy prescriptions are advocated with the same lack of success. It is from this profound dissatisfaction with the subject of economics that this book has sprung. It represents a personal attempt to come to terms with the limitations of economic theory and to offer a way forward. It is a book founded on the belief that we should never accept any problem as insoluble. Mass unemployment is not a natural and inevitable phenomenon beyond our control. To treat it as such severely restricts our understanding and, above all, it denies hope. This book seeks an alternative understanding of the operation of the capitalist economy which provides a more adequate explanation of mass unemployment and a more effective set of policy prescriptions.

This book is founded on the proposition that the problems with orthodox economic theory are primarily the result of the particular ideas which economists have about the nature and status of their theories. Orthodox economists have adopted a methodological stance which denies any limitations to the ability of orthodox economic theory to explain economic phenomena. This methodological stance has led generations of theoretical economists to construct a highly elaborate theory of the capitalist economy which is at variance with actual experience. Orthodox economic theory reaches theoretical deductions which are claimed to be of practical relevance. This book is a plea for theoretical economists to question the assumed authority of orthodox economic theory, to define the limits of its relevance and to develop alternative, non-orthodox theories to deal with those aspects of economic phenomena for which orthodox theories are deemed irrelevant. Thus this book represents a plea for revolutionary changes in the methodology of economics. Such changes are a necessary prerequisite for any adequate reconstruction of economic theory.

The concern with the simple, basic ideas underlying economic theory has dictated the particular, non-conventional style of discourse adopted in the book. First, there is no attempt in the text to relate the present analysis to the existing body of economic theory in any detailed, author-by-author manner. The objective is to convey an impression of a whole view. References to the existing literature would detract from this impressionist approach. Hence such references have been omitted from the main text and are contained instead in an appendix on the sources and influences of the present analysis. A second departure from the normal style of discourse in economic theory is the almost complete lack of any mathematical presentation of the arguments. Again, this is a reflection of the fact that the concern of the present analysis is at a very fundamental level of the subject. The problem lies not with the logical and mathematical methods of economic theory as such but with the starting-points, the premises from which deductions are drawn. However, there is another reason for not using mathematical forms of presentation. There has been a long-standing tendency in economic theory to choose assumptions to facilitate the use of mathematical methods. The nature of the particular object of analysis should determine the choice of the appropriate technique of analysis, rather than, as is the case in economics, a particular technique of analysis determining the nature of the specified object of analysis. If ever there was a case of the tail wagging the proverbial dog, it is the misuse of mathematics in economics. The present analysis puts a priority on the specification of the object of analysis. The deduction of the detailed implications of the particular specification presented here is an important but subsequent task in which mathematical methods will inevitably have a role. That is how it should be.

This text draws on a number of personal insights inspired by a number of sources. The most significant of these influences is Keynes's *General Theory*. Keynes's writing have been the main catalyst for the development of the present analysis. Inevitably this means that the present analysis contains an implied interpretation of Keynes's *General Theory*. However, the academic question concerning the validity of this implied interpretation of Keynes is peripheral with regard to the principal objectives of this work. The ideas presented should be judged primarily on the grounds of whether or not they provide an acceptable theory of the operation of the capitalist economy.

If a label is needed this book should be considered as post-classical. It accepts that classical theory, the orthodox approach in economic theory, is valid within certain clearly defined limits to its relevance. However, beyond these limits, alternative, non-classical approaches must be developed. In particular, Keynes's theory of employment offers the appropriate, non-classical starting-point for understanding the operation of the industrial sector in the capitalist economy. The present analysis is revolutionary inasmuch and it is intended to be a move beyond the confines of orthodoxy. Thus, at times, it is very critical and dismissive of that orthodoxy where it has been extended beyond what should be the limits to its relevance. But the message of the post-classical approach is essentially conciliatory. Economic theory can, and indeed must, overcome the qualitative fragmentation between different schools of thought, a situation in which each school considers itself to be in sole possession of the single legitimate approach to understanding economic phenomena. The post-classical approach offers a way forward.

Sir Isaiah Berlin once made the famous distinction between writers who are hedgehogs and others who are foxes. Quite unashamedly I admit that this book is the work of a hedgehog who considers himself to be in possession of one big idea. It is a big idea but a very simple and obvious one. Perhaps it would seem less simple and obvious if I had been more attached to orthodox economic theory. If the basic approach presented here can be accepted, the foxes may then get to work with filling in the details.

1

Introduction

The nature of theory

The object of theory is to explain why things are as they are. Theory is a means of providing order by discovering the principles and laws which underlie observed phenomena. Theory seeks to find patterns in a world of seemingly chaotic appearance, to create order out of chaos. This search for order has led to the creation of theoretical systems which attempt to explain every aspect of observed phenomena. Traditionally each theoretical system is treated as objective and exclusive, the only value-free way of viewing the particular aspect of the world with which it is concerned. It is this status of objectivity on which the authority of any particular theoretical system is founded.

Objectivity is usually claimed on behalf of a theoretical system on the basis of an adherence to the scientific method. In particular, the proponents of a theoretical system tend to lay claim to the falsificationist view of science associated with the writings of Karl Popper. The falsificationist view of science sees scientists as continually searching for empirical evidence with which to falsify the current provisionally held theories. Thus scientific knowledge, at any point in time, is seen to consist of those conjectures which have not yet been refuted by empirical testing. It is empirical testing which is seen to play the crucial role in the scientific process, providing the objective standard with which to judge theories. Science is a rational process, progressing towards objective truth on the basis of the falsificationist method of theory selection. It is the empirical testing of theories which is the distinguishing characteristic of science, the demarcation criterion which separates the sciences from the value-ridden non-sciences.

It is accepted that there are problems associated with the

falsificationist method. The so-called Duhem–Quine thesis holds that it is difficult, if not impossible, to refute theories completely since testing always involves more than a single target hypothesis. Any empirical test always involves the target hypothesis in conjunction with a whole set of auxiliary hypotheses. It follows, therefore, that any refutation is a refutation of only a particular conjunction of hypotheses, not of the target hypothesis. This creates the possibility that any theory could be rendered consistent with the available empirical evidence through the appropriate revision of the auxiliary hypotheses. The existence of auxiliary hypotheses means that there are always potential immunizing stratagems at hand to counter any negative empirical results. It follows, therefore, that the empirical testing of theories is not a purely objective process.

The Duhem–Quine thesis casts into doubt the proposition that science is an objective means towards knowledge. Indeed, in recent years the adequacy of the traditional view of science has been increasingly questioned by a number of philosophers of science who have recognized that there is much more to science than allowed for by the falsificationist picture. The key contribution to this 'new view' of science is Kuhn's theory of scientific revolutions. Kuhn sees science as operating within paradigms which contain the fundamental world-view shared by the members of a particular scientific community. According to Kuhn, normal science occurs when the majority of scientists within a particular scientific community accept a single paradigm and attempt to develop theories within the paradigm to account for more and more observed phenomena. Kuhn sees science as exhibiting long periods of stability, characterized by the development of normal science. These periods of stability are interrupted by periods of crisis, when the dominant paradigm fails to explain important anomalies. One rare outcome of such scientific crises is the replacement of the existing paradigm by a new paradigm, a process which Kuhn describes as a scientific revolution. Thus the development of science is not a continuous evolutionary process but is one punctuated by revolutionary changes in the way scientists view the world.

The ideas of Kuhn, amongst others, have led to the development of what could be called a 'new view' of science which rejects the notion that science is objective. The traditional view claims that science is an objective, value-free process, this objectivity deriving from the empirical testing of theories. The 'new view' of science begins from the premise that the way scientists view the world depends on their underlying frame of reference, the particular set of presupposed notions of order which they adopt, often unwittingly. It is this set of presuppositions which Kuhn described as a paradigm. These presuppositions can be seen as representing what Polanyi described as a tacit dimension of knowledge, rarely, if ever, formulated and rarely discussed. Scientific theories are interpretations of the world relative to a particular frame of reference. The result of scientific investigations is consistency between theories and empirical evidence within a frame of reference. It follows, therefore, that science is not objective. The myth of objectivity is perpetuated by the bounded vision of scientists who fail to acknowledge that the way they see things currently is only one amongst many. The myth of objectivity is dangerous and misleading, blinding scientists to the existence of an inescapable metaphysical dimension to their theories. It is the achievement of the 'new view' of science to have shown that there is no Archimedean point by which to lift science into the rarefied realms of objectivity.

The 'new view' of science recognizes that science is a social process in which the objective is to attain a consensus within any particular scientific community. It should not be inferred from this that anything goes when it comes to scientific knowledge provided it is agreed upon within the scientific community. A necessary condition for the maintenance of a particular theoretical system is its continued ability to achieve consistency between theory and empirical evidence. But consistency is not a sufficient condition to determine the particular form of the theoretical system currently held by a scientific community. Any theoretical system is dependent on the social context of which it is part and the historical process from which it has emerged. The point is that there are no bare facts against which theories can be objectively judged. The facts depend on the frames of reference within which they must necessarily exist. These frames of reference, in turn, are the product of historical experience. The facts of nature influence our theories but always in a way that we ourselves mediate.

One of the basic presuppositions common to almost all scientific communities is the reductionist notion that all phenomena within a particular field of investigation can be explained ultimately with reference to some single set of first principles. This produces closed theoretical systems in which there is no recognition of any limitations to the relevance of the particular frame of reference adopted. These closed theoretical systems take on an ever-evolving pyramidal structure as the set of first principles are elaborated and applied to an increasing range of observed phenomena. When combined with the belief in objectivity, the reductionist method can lead to the qualitative fragmentation of particular scientific communities. Different schools of thought may emerge within the same subject field, each with a very different frame of reference. Qualitative fragmentation occurs as a result of each school of thought believing its own frame of reference to be the only correct, value-free way of viewing the world. The existence of a multitude of closed theoretical systems within the same subject field breeds an atmosphere of intolerance, since every school deems only its approach to be legitimate. The fragmentation is increased as each school develops its own language. Communication between schools is rendered almost impossible since no common ground exists for such interaction. Drawing on the philosophy of Wittgenstein, it can be said that within any subject a number of different language-games are being played simultaneously by the different schools of thought. The players recognize the legitimacy of the rules of their own language-game only; the language-games of others are dismissed as meaningless.

The reductionist method involves a particular restrictive presupposition about the nature of the underlying order within the world. It is a presupposition of a purely metaphysical nature, a matter of belief which can never itself be subject to proof or disproof. The scientific revolutions highlighted by Kuhn leave the reductionist presupposition unchallenged. One closed theoretical system is replaced by another. An alternative, more general, presupposition is that phenomena should be viewed as pluralist in nature. This implies the acceptance of what could be termed the principle of complementarity. No single frame of reference is seen as being capable of providing on its own an adequate understanding of any particular phenomena. Rather, there is a need to develop alternative, complementary frames of reference. The limits to the relevance of particular frames of reference are defined and the interconnections between different frames of reference are explored. This pluralist method leads to the development of open theoretical systems. There is a recognition of the need to combine the two activities of what Bohm has called adaptation and perception. Adaptation involves the development of the implications of a particular set of pre-existing notions of order, while perception involves the creation of new notions of order. Both activities are necessary elements of a pluralist approach.

The adoption of this method offers a means to overcome the qualitative fragmentation and intolerance which prevails within some scientific communities. It also entails a methodological revolution going far beyond the scientific revolutions described by Kuhn. This methodological revolution involves an acceptance that different notions of order are legitimate within the same subject field. Different schools of thought need to interact, in a co-operative manner, to determine the limits to the meaningfulness of the different language-games. Each school must learn the grammar of the language-games of other schools. This is not to say that science should be free of conflict. Far from it. Science requires the critical tension created by different ideas. The point is that this intellectual conflict should take place within an atmosphere of tolerance and open-mindedness.

The state of modern economic theory

Modern economic theory is dominated by a single approach, that of classical theory. It is an approach adhered to by the majority of economists. Classical theory provides most economists with their basic simple ideas with which they seek to explain economic behaviour. Classical theory has not been some unchanging monolith during its reign over the last 200 years; far from it. There has been a progressive evolution during its development with the result that it has undergone much radical change in its theoretical forms. In particular, the so-called marginalist revolution of the 1870s marked the transformation from the early classical form of Smith and Ricardo to the later neoclassical form which remains dominant to this day. Despite such radical changes at the level of theory, there has been a continuity at the most fundamental level with regard to the basic vision of the economy. Smith's famous notion of the price mechanism acting as an invisible hand ensuring order in the economic sphere of activity, still holds sway over the hearts and minds of the majority within the economics profession. The language may have changed but the message remains the same.

Classical theory is treated by its followers as the only objective approach to the study of economic behaviour. Indeed, classical theory is described within its own textbooks as positive, value-free economics. This objectivity is claimed on the basis that (classical) economics is a science, adhering to the methods of falsificationism. Classical theories, it is claimed, have successfully survived the rigours of empirical testing. Whether or not econometrics provides a means of critical testing on a par with the experimental methods of the more exact natural sciences, is an open question, as evidenced by the continuing debate over the scientific standing of economics. Yet the degree to which economics follows the methods of fasificationism is not really the crucial question. The 'Is economics a science?' debate is in many respects a secondary one which deflects argument away from what should be the primary focus of attention. That focus of attention should be the methodological stance adopted by the followers of classical theory. It is not the validity of the claim to be scientific which is important but rather the implications of making the claim in the first place. By adopting the traditional view of science, the followers of classical theory blind themselves to the possibility of any limitations to the relevance of classical theory in explaining all aspects of economic behaviour. Classical theory is not recognized as the product of a particular frame of reference, a particular set of presupposed notions of order. It is the methodological stance adopted by the followers of classical theory which has created the bounded vision so pervasive in modern economic theory.

Classical theory may be the dominant orthodoxy within economic theory, but it is far from being a universally accepted one. There have always been a significant number of economists who have rejected classical theory as the appropriate starting-point for understanding economic behaviour. Probably the most important of these heretics was John Maynard Keynes. In his book, *The General Theory of Employment, Interest and Money*, Keynes claimed to have rejected classical theory. The basis of this claim was Keynes's belief that he had developed a theory of involuntary unemployment, a type of unemployment beyond the classical frame of reference. Involuntary unemployment belonged to a new frame of reference, a concept whose meaning could only be understood within a new language-game. Keynes's claim to have broken away from classical theory has inspired a large number of economists and continues to do so. The search is on for a Keynesian frame of reference with which to provide a coherent alternative theoretical system.

The response of some orthodox (classical) economists to Keynes's challenge has been to interpret *The General Theory* in terms of the classical frame of reference. This has led to the emergence of what can be called classical Keynesianism. Classical Keynesianism is an attempt to incorporate Keynes's ideas within classical theory. It seeks to create an orthodox synthesis which integrates Keynes's macroeconomics with classical microfoundations. Such an orthodox synthesis denies that Keynes made any fundamental break with classical theory. Rather Keynes's *General Theory* is seen as dealing with what was at the time a relatively underdeveloped area within classical theory on the behaviour of the macro economy. In this way Keynes's *General Theory* has come to be used as a catalyst towards the further elaboration of classical macroeconomics. Far from breaking away from classical theory, classical Keynesianism has opened up a series of new developments within it.

Classical Keynesianism represents one of the three main schools of thought within modern classical macroeconomics. The other two mains schools of thought are the neoclassical/monetarist school and the more recent new classical school. These three classical schools of thought share the same set of presuppositions about the fundamental nature of the macro economy. All operate wholly within the classical frame of reference. They differ only with respect to the particular lines of thought which they develop within that frame of reference. The divisions between these classical schools represent a quantitative fragmentation of the subject field; a fragmentation at the level of theory rather than at a more fundamental level. Furthermore, it is a fragmentation which could, at least in principle, be resolved through empirical testing given the acceptance of a common frame of reference.

This fragmentation within the subject field of economics goes beyond the quantitative fragmentation between the classical schools of thought. As has already been said, there has always been a significant number of economists working outside the orthodox citadel. In recent times many of these heretics have been Keynesians who have denied the validity of the classical Keynesian interpretation of Keynes's *General Theory*. These heretical Keynesians form a very diverse and loose grouping known collectively as the post-Keynesians. They seek to interpret Keynes in terms of a non-orthodox frame of reference. Not surprisingly, there is little in the way of agreement between post-Keynesians about the appropriate non-orthodox setting for Keynes's insights. As with most heretics and revolutionaries, agreement between them begins and ends with their rejection of what has gone before. Beyond that common starting-point there is little else in the way of coherence. The post-Keynesian school is characterized by a number of competing sub-schools. Amongst the more prominent of these sub-schools are the fundamentalists, who stress the importance of time and uncertainty; the neo-Ricardians, who wish to integrate Keynes's macro theory with the early classical theories of value and distribution; the Chapter 17 Keynesians, who focus on the monetary aspects of the *General Theory*; and the post-Kaleckians, who believe that Kalecki's independent discovery of the same insights as Keynes provides a more satisfactory approach, since Kalecki based his analysis quite explicitly on the non-orthodox microfoundations of imperfect competition and mark-up pricing. These four post-Keynesian sub-schools are by no means the only ones, just the most prominent among many. Each has tended to highlight only one aspect of Keynes's work to the exclusion of all others. Many could be considered as complementary, although some do offer irreconcilable alternatives. The most significant example of these deep divisions is the denial by the neo-Ricardians of anything but a peripheral, even irrelevant, role to Keynes's discussions of the effects of uncertainty, in complete contrast to the fundamentalists, who view this aspect as the real essence of Keynes's *General Theory*. The divisions within often run as deep as the divisions between the post-Keynesian school and the classical school in its various forms.

The post-Keynesians represent one amongst several strands of opposition to the classical orthodoxy. The Marxist school is another, with a far longer-standing tradition within economics. The writings of the institutionalists also continue to be a source of critique and inspiration towards an alternative. The result is that the subject field of economics is characterized by qualitative fragmentation to a very significant extent. Adherents of a particular frame of reference deem only their own approach to be objective and, hence, legitimate. All other approaches are rejected as value-ridden and non-scientific. This breeds an atmosphere of intense intolerance. Communication between schools is limited and often characterized by purely polemical attacks on each other. Such an intellectual stalemate is almost an inevitable outcome when qualitative fragmentation exists. Each school sees only its own approach as necessary for a full understanding of economic behaviour. Thus there is no need for any dialogue between schools. Furthermore, there is no means for such a dialogue since there is no common set of presupposed notions of order on which to base meaningful communication. Each school has its own language, its own concepts, its own meanings. The state of modern economic theory has much in common with the biblical Tower of Babel.

The problem of incommensurability is most evident with regard to the debate over the use of the mathematical mode of discourse. For those within the classical approach, mathematics provides a powerful language with which to deduce the logical implications of classical theory. From this viewpoint, the opponents of mathematical (classical) economics are intellectual philistines who wish to return economics to the pre-scientific dark ages. But there are very legitimate sources of concern about the use of mathematics in economics. Mathematical economics can be regarded as an extremely elegant and sophisticated superstructure built on very shaky foundations. It is not the use of mathematics as such which is the problem. Mathematics is, after all, a very powerful means of logical deduction. The problem with the mathematical mode of discourse is its tendency to obscure the need to question the presuppositions which underlie the mathematical models. Mathematical economists just get on with the job-in-hand with little or no debate about their starting-point. They have a map and a destination, so why waste time debating; 'get going' is the motto. It is this lack of critical evaluation of the basic axioms of orthodox theory which is the root cause of much of the controversy in modern economic theory. The blind acceptance of the usefulness of mathematics has tended to lead economists to choose their concepts and assumptions on the basis of the requirements of mathematical techniques rather than the choice of technique being determined by the nature of the phenomena to be studied. Another case of the tail wagging the dog. The assumption of the rational economic agent is the prime example of a technique-generated assumption, allowing as it does the use of constrained optimization methods. It is concerns such as these which have led many to question the empirical relevance of the highly abstract mathematical models so much in vogue within economics in recent years. But for those operating within the mathematical mode of discourse, such concerns have little validity. The inevitable result is that each side of this intellectual divide accuses the other of failing to understand the role of mathematics in economics.

Mass unemployment

There are at least two very different aspects to human knowledge: the scientific aspect and the technological aspect. The scientific aspect involves the search for explanation, the creation of order out of chaos. The technological aspect, on the other hand, concerns the provision of the ability to change the environment. The scientific aspect of knowledge attempts to satisfy the deep-rooted human need for certainty, whereas the technological aspect attempts to satisfy the need for control. These twin aspects of knowledge are inextricably linked. The explanations provided by the scientific aspect necessarily influence the prescriptions of the technological aspect. Where you want to go is always partly determined by your map of where you are. Thus competing theoretical systems may offer competing technological prescriptions. Different notions of order can imply different means of control.

The single most important task facing economic theory is to explain the causes of mass unemployment. Capitalist economies appear to be prone to recurrent bouts of mass unemployment in which vast numbers of individuals are deprived of their only possible source of an adequate income. Economic theory needs to explain why this happens so that the appropriate policy responses may be devised.

Capitalist economies experienced mass unemployment during the inter-war years. At that time orthodox economic opinion advocated *laissez-faire* prescriptions. Classical theory viewed the capitalist economy as a self-regulating system which would automatically adjust itself towards a full-employment equilibrium. Hence it followed that there was no need for government intervention to manage the economy. At most, economic policy should involve only temporary interventions if the adjustment processes were operating too slowly.

In *The General Theory* Keynes attacked this orthodox analysis. Keynes seemed to provide the theoretical justification for permanent government intervention on the grounds that the economy would not automatically ensure a full-employment equilibrium. Thus the followers of Keynes advocated that governments should use central controls to manage the economic system in order to maintain full employment. This was the Keynesian revolution in policy.

The 1970s and 1980s have witnessed another period of mass unemployment in the capitalist economies. This has gone hand-in-hand with a classical counter-revolution within economics. Governments have adopted the policy prescriptions of the monetarist and new classical schools. These schools are advocates of pre-Keynesian, *laissez-faire* policies, albeit in more sophisticated modern forms. Economic policy has come full circle.

The success of the classical counter-revolution has been aided, in part, by the inadequacies of the theoretical foundations of Keynesian thought. The fragmentation of Keynesian theory has seriously undermined the position of Keynesian policy prescriptions. The emergence of classical Keynesianism, incorporating Keynesian ideas within classical theory, has led, almost inevitably, to doubts about the efficacy of Keynesian policy. The failure of post-Keynesian theory to provide a coherent and widely accepted alternative analysis has further weakened the case for an activist policy stance.

The bounded vision in modern economic theory is more than just a methodological and theoretical problem. It has contributed towards millions of individuals living in social and economic poverty as the result of prolonged periods of mass unemployment. These are the victims of the orthodox economic doctrines which deny the hope of any macro policy solutions. It must be the task of economists to question continually these orthodox beliefs. There is an obligation to do so.

A way forward

This book sets itself the theoretical task of trying to offer a way forward for economic theory out of its intellectual stalemate. By overcoming the bounded vision and qualitative fragmentation so prevalent in modern economic theory, economics will be enabled to provide the policy prescriptions so urgently required. The theoretical task is by no means a sufficient condition for the solution of our economic ills. But it seems certain that a more adequate economic theory is a necessary condition.

The starting-point for the way forward advocated here is the realization that the problems within modern economic theory stem from the simple basic ideas which underlie it. In particular, the deep divisions within modern economic theory are the result of the methodological stance adopted by most economists, often implicitly. Economists tend to adopt a method which is reductionist and objectivist. Most economists operate within a particular set of presupposed notions of order: the classical frame of reference. This particular perception of economic phenomena is treated as objective and value-free, the only legitimate way of seeing the world. This belief in the objectivity of classical theory is justified by adherence to the traditional (falsificationist) view of science. No limitations are recognized to the ability of classical theory to provide a full explanation of economic phenomena. This methodological stance inevitably results in the qualitative fragmentation within the subject field of economics between the classical school and other schools of thought offering alternative and equally closed theoretical systems. Each school sees itself as having the only truly objective and legitimate approach to the study of economic phenomena.

The way forward in economics requires as a first step that economists become aware of the nature of their theories. In particular, there is a need to recognize explicitly the inevitability of a metaphysical dimension to their knowledge. This is one of the principal propositions of the 'new view' of science. The recognition of the existence of a metaphysical dimension to knowledge would allow economists to see objectivity for the myth that it is. It would also allow economists to see the reductionist approach as a particular and highly restrictive view of the nature of order. A more general and open view of the nature of order is the pluralist one based on the presupposition that phenomena may require to be explained in terms of qualitatively different types of order. This pluralist view of order necessitates the development of alternative but complementary frames of reference. This more general form of presupposition allows for the reductionist view as a special case which may or may not be appropriate for particular phenomena. The pluralist approach means that economists would no longer attempt to force the world of economic phenomena into a one-dimensional strait-jacket. But the adoption of the multi-dimensional pluralist approach would involve a methodological revolution going beyond a Kuhnian scientific revolution. It is not the replacement of one closed theoretical system by another closed system that is required, but the move to an open theoretical system incorporating many different frames of reference.

In economics the methodological revolution requires an awareness of the possibility of limitations to the relevance of the classical frame of reference. The classical frame of reference needs to be seen as relevant to one particular dimension of economic phenomena, a dimension which will later be described as the allocative mode of activity. However, once the pluralist approach is adopted, it is no longer the case that all economic phenomena should be presupposed to be allocative. Thus economists must seek to define the limitations to the relevance of the classical frame of reference, to develop alternative but complementary frames of reference to deal with the non-allocative aspects of economic phenomena, and to discover the interconnections between these different aspects. This is the essence of the post-classical approach. It calls for a revolutionary synthesis between what have been seen previously as irreconcilable alternatives.

The post-classical approach, as developed here, owes much to the writings of Keynes. His insights have been one of the main influences in its development. Why then have I used the label post-classical rather than post-Keynesian, particularly since many post-Keynesians would embrace much of the interpretation of Keynes's *General Theory* implied by the present analysis? There are two main reasons for the claim to be post-classical rather than post-Keynesian. First, and most importantly, the post-classical approach is explicitly founded on a particular methodological stance. To be post-classical is to adopt a pluralist conception of economic phenomena. However, within the post-Keynesian school, such methodological issues have been relegated to a secondary, almost a peripheral, importance, and indeed, many post-Keynesians adopt the same methodological stance as the followers of classical theory. A second reason why the approach on offer is more appropriately called post-classical is the explicit recognition that classical theory has validity as a theory of allocation, one particular aspect of economic phenomena. The revolutionary break from classical theory is not to deny it completely, as some post-Keynesians have a tendency to do, but rather to recognize that there are very significant limitations to its relevance. It is not completely wrong but neither is it completely right. It is one dimension of a multi-dimensional world. The post-classical approach offers a synthesis of classical and non-classical theories as a means of moving beyond the qualitative fragmentation of modern economic theory, a fragmentation which the post-Keynesian school has tended to intensify rather than overcome.

The post-classical approach offers a way forward for economics. The implied methodological revolution would allow the development of more general theories of economic phenomena. Economists must come to terms with the nature of their own theories. Economists, like all scientists, always work within webs of significance, albeit very sophisticated ones, which they themselves spin. You cannot escape from such webs but you can escape from the bounded vision created by the failure to recognize the constraints inherent in any particular set of presupposed notions of order. Such a critical awareness of the nature and status of economic theories offers a more secure basis for their future development. Too often economists profess dogmatic truths, the authority of which rests on nothing more than the myth of objectivity. Economists must accept, and come to terms with, the realization that economics can never be an objective truth. The authority of economics is the responsibility of economists themselves. The post-classical approach offers a means of responding to this loss of certainty.

A theory of the capitalist economy: an outline

This book is concerned primarily with the simple basic ideas which underlie economic theory. Those working within classical theory have developed the logical implications of their fundamental axioms in much detail and with great elegance and formality. It is not this process of deduction with which I take issue. Rather, it is the lack of critical evaluation of the axioms themselves. This book sets out to provide just such a critical evaluation and is therefore based, first and foremost, on intuition, not logical deduction. This is not to say that logical deduction has no role. An attempt is made to detail some of the logical implications which follow from the approach adopted. This is a necessary part of the analysis. But it is the simple basic ideas on which the book, ultimately, must be judged.

The objective is to introduce the idea of a post-classical approach as a way forward for economic theory. It is readily and repeatedly admitted that there is no attempt to work out fully the detailed implications of such a post-classical approach – clearly an impossible task. Rather, the aim is to suggest the possibilities which the post-classical approach opens up. This is done by readdressing one particular question, namely the question posed by Keynes's *General Theory*: what is the short-run macro behaviour of a closed capitalist economy? This question is the focus of attention for this particular volume. It implies, therefore, that there is no systematic treatment of all the micro aspects of economic phenomena but only those which are of particular relevance to the short-run macro concerns of the present analysis. Nor is there any examination of the implications of the longer-run effects of changes in the capital stock or the implications of the internationalization of economic processes. A further limitation is the concentration on the economic aspects only of the behaviour of the capitalist economy to the exclusion of the equally important non-economic aspects. These are all important issues which deserve detailed analysis in their own right. This book concentrates only on Keynes's original question as a means of introducing the post-classical approach. Keynes's original question has been, after all, the dominant concern of modern macroeconomic theory. The answers proposed for this particular question are suggestive for the analysis of the other important issues not dealt with directly in the present analysis. Furthermore, if the post-classical approach can aid the development of a more adequate understanding of the economic aspect, it will have made a significant contribution to the development of the political economy of capitalism in which the non-economic aspects would be given due consideration. Thus the aims can be summed up best by an old Chinese proverb which teaches that a thousand-mile journey begins with a single step. This book tries to take the first faltering step on what will be, hopefully, a long but fruitful journey of discovery for economic theory in future years.

A start is made with an attempt to clarify the nature of ortho-dox (classical) economic theory by examining its presupposed notions of order. Chapter 2 argues that classical theory adopts a frame of reference within which the capitalist economy is viewed as an exchange economy. All economic behaviour is treated as an allocative process of stock adjustment regulated by the price mechanism. It is the macro properties of an exchange economy which have been logically deduced by the classical Keynesian, neoclassical/monetarist and new classical schools of thought. In particular, these classical schools of thought accept that the price mechanism can ensure a perfect allocative equilibrium of gener-alized market-clearing provided that certain structural and infor-mational conditions are met. At the macro level, this translates into the proposition that the exchange economy will adjust auto-matically to a full-employment equilibrium. Starting from this basic proposition, the different macro-orientated classical schools have derived various imperfectionist theories of macro misalloca-tion in which the effects of structural and informational imperfec-tions have been examined with particular reference to the causation of unemployment.

Classical theory is a closed theoretical system which adopts one particular frame of reference. It is possible to view economic phenomena from the standpoint of alternative, non-classical frames of reference. Chapter 3 considers one such alternative. It explores the nature of a monetary production economy. This is an alternative conceptualization of the economic system which rec-ognizes the existence of non-allocative modes of activity. In particular, the monetary context of behaviour is viewed as imply-ing that output and employment, at the macro level, are not determined by a price mechanism but by the non-allocative multiplier process. This theory of a monetary production econ-omy is inspired to a great extent by Keynes's *General Theory*. However, it is important to note, with respect to the theory of a monetary production economy presented here, that its validity, as an implied interpretation of Keynes, is peripheral to the objectives of the present analysis. The sole concern of this book is with the question of whether or not the theory of a monetary production economy can contribute towards the development of a more general theory of economic phenomena.

The fundamental argument is that the economic aspect of the capitalist economy can be dealt with adequately only by a theoretical system consisting of alternative, but complementary, frames of reference. This is the pluralist presupposition underlying the post-classical approach. When applied to Keynes's original question about the short-run macro properties of a closed economy, the post-classical approach results in a dualist conceptualization of the capitalist economy. The dualist nature of the capitalist economy arises from the different behavioural processes exhibited by the industrial sector and the financial sector. Chapter 4 provides a theory of the capitalist economy in which the monetary production economy is used as the starting-point for the analysis of the industrial sector, while the classical theory of the exchange economy provides the starting-point for the analysis of the financial sector. In this way a post-classical synthesis is developed between a reformulated classical theory with clearly defined limitations to its relevance, and an alternative non-classical frame of reference derived from Keynes.

Some of the implications of this post-classical theory of the capitalist economy are developed in chapters 5 and 6. Chapter 5 provides a more detailed treatment of the financial sector, with particular reference to differences and interconnections between the banking and stock-market systems. The banking system is viewed as part of the monetary production economy, characterized primarily by non-allocative patterns of behaviour. The stock-market system, on the other hand, is primarily allocative in nature but with significant non-allocative features. Chapter 5 also provides a preliminary outline of the interaction between the industrial and financial sectors. Chapter 6 develops the post-classical approach with respect to the problems of unemployment and inflation, showing the highly restrictive nature of the explanations provided by classical theory. The famous Phillips curve debate is reassessed in the light of the post-classical approach, leading to an outline of some of the implications of the post-classical analysis for macroeconomic policy prescription.

The arguments are provocative and intentionally so. It is hoped to get economists thinking about their traditional presuppositions. No doubt this will generate hostility from some. But for those who are willing and open-minded, this book may prove to be a catalyst and inspiration towards the theoretical developments so urgently required – the first step on a thousand-mile journey.

2

The Exchange Economy

Classical theory

The dominant orthodoxy in economic thought is classical theory. Classical theory attempts to explain all economic phenomena in terms of one single frame of reference, the classical frame of reference. It is this frame of reference which is shared by the three main schools of thought within classical macroeconomic theory – the neoclassical/monetarist school, the classical Keynesian school and the new classical school. The classical frame of reference views the capitalist economy as an exchange economy made up of a series of markets in which commodities are traded. This is the market-theoretic dimension of the classical frame of reference. The whole of classical theory flows from this basic market-theoretic presupposition about the nature of the capitalist economy. Classical theory is a theory of the properties exhibited by an exchange economy.

Within an exchange economy all economic behaviour consists of the voluntary exchange of commodities through markets. Economic agents possess stocks of commodities which they are prepared to exchange in order to obtain a more preferred stock holding. Classical theory is a theory of this process of stock adjustment. Agents must choose how much to trade at the prevailing terms of exchange. Economic agents are assumed to be rational in the sense of making optimizing choices. This assumption represents the choice-theoretic dimension of the classical frame of reference. Rational economic agents maximize their welfare by trading each commodity up to the point at which the benefits from further trade are just equalled by the costs incurred.

In a pure exchange economy agents trade the existing stocks of commodities. The existence of production does not alter the nature of the exchange economy in any fundamental way. Firms exist in order to transform physically certain commodities in the production process to create other, more desirable, commodities. Firms behave in a similar way to all other agents, engaging in exchange with the objective of maximizing their welfare. In the case of firms, the objective is profit maximization. Firms buy the factors of production supplied by households and other firms, producing products which are, in turn, demanded by households and other firms.

In an exchange economy the process of stock adjustment is conducted within markets. Markets are regulated by the price mechanism. This process is explained by the demand-and-supply theory of price determination, the theoretical core of orthodox economics. If the price mechanism is able to operate freely and efficiently, the market price of a commodity moves to the market-clearing level, at which the total quantity of the commodity demanded equals the total quantity supplied. At this point all agents are able to fulfil their desired trading plans at the prevailing price. They therefore have no incentive to alter their behaviour. Hence the market is in equilibrium, a position in which it remains in the absence of any external shocks. Classical theory seeks to determine the nature of the equilibrium outcome. This is the equilibrium-theoretic dimension of the classical frame of reference. The effects of any external shocks are investigated by comparing the equilibrium outcomes before and after the shock. This is the method of comparative statics.

The price mechanism ensures an automatic tendency for the market price to move to a market-clearing equilibrium. If the market price is above the market-clearing level, there is excess supply, with sellers willing to supply more than buyers are prepared to purchase. This is a disequilibrium position which induces changes in agent behaviour. Sellers tend to lower the price and the quantity supplied in order to prevent themselves from being left with unsold stocks. The fall in price tends to stimulate demand. Eventually the market price falls to its market-clearing level. Similarly, if the market price is below the market-clearing level, there is excess demand. This disequilibrium tends to lead sellers to increase the price and the quantity supplied, leading again, to a convergence towards the equilibrium market-clearing price.

The demand-and-supply theory of price determination means that prices and quantities are determined simultaneously by market forces. Prices and quantities are entirely interdependent, the joint outcomes of the same behavioural process. This behavioural process is the process of allocation. Classical theory is, essentially, a theory of the allocative mode of activity. Price plays the purely allocative role of ensuring equality between market demand and supply during the process of stock adjustment through exchange. If the price mechanism is able to operate efficiently in a market, it ensures the achievement of an allocative equilibrium.

The demand-and-supply theory of price determination implies a static analysis of price in the sense that the current equilibrium level of price depends solely on the current levels of demand and supply. Past levels of price have no influence whatsoever on the current equilibrium level of price. Such dynamic factors are only relevant in the analysis of market disequilibrium as price adjusts towards the market-clearing equilibrium. This static conception of economic phenomena is inevitable given the equilibrium-theoretic presupposition within the classical frame of reference.

If the price mechanism is able to operate efficiently throughout the economy, this creates a tendency for an exchange economy to move towards a general (allocative) equilibrium in which all markets clear. Every agent is able to trade the desired quantity of every commodity at the prevailing set of market prices. This, in turn, means that welfare in the economy as a whole is maximized, given the initial distribution of endowments. Hence the free operation of the price mechanism produces an economic optimum in which resources are utilized efficiently to maximize economic welfare. This is the invisible-hand theorem. The price mechanism acts as an invisible hand supposedly ensuring that within the economic sphere the pursuit of individual self-interest brings about the best of all possible worlds. This invisible-hand theorem represents the central and by far the most significant proposition of classical theory with an immense influence way beyond the confines of economic theory. It is a proposition which has become an article of faith for all those who profess classical free-market liberalism, the dominant political ideology of our times.

Say's Law

Say's Law states that supply creates its own demand. Classical theory shows that Say's Law is a fundamental property of the macro exchange economy in equilibrium. The macro exchange economy tends to generate sufficient aggregate demand to support the equilibrium level of aggregate supply. This implies that classical theory is a supply-side economics since the supply-side is the driving force within the macro exchange economy, ultimately determining the point of equilibrium for the whole economy.

Within the market-theoretic approach of classical theory the supply-side in the short-run is conceived of as a labour market in which the level of employment (and hence the level of output) and the real wage are determined simultaneously by the forces of demand and supply. The classical theory of the labour market is an application of the demand-and-supply theory of price determination. Under conditions of perfect competition profit-maximizing firms employ labour up to the point at which the marginal product of labour equals the real wage. Under the additional assumption that labour exhibits diminishing marginal productivity, the demand for labour varies inversely with the real wage. Thus an increase in the level of employment requires a fall in the real wage. The supply of labour by households is usually assumed to vary directly with the real wage. This is justified in terms of a work–leisure trade-off in which households are viewed as allocating their time between work and leisure. The real wage measures the opportunity cost of substituting leisure for work. It is normally assumed that a rise in the real wage will lead households to allocate more time to work since the opportunity cost of leisure time will be higher. If market forces are able to operate freely and efficiently in the labour market, the real wage moves to the market-clearing level. The equilibrium outcome in the labour market is full employment; there are sufficient jobs on offer to employ all those seeking work at the prevailing real wage. Thus, on the supply-side, the price mechanism moves the macro exchange economy to a full-employment level of output.

The classical theory of the labour market implies that the real wage and the level of employment are determined simultaneously, the joint outcomes of the allocative process. This means that the wage bargain between employers and employees to set the money wage is wholly determined by the forces of demand and supply. The money wage is set such that, given the price level, the resulting real wage is at the market-clearing level.

For the macro exchange economy to be in equilibrium, there

must be sufficient aggregate demand to purchase the aggregate supply of output. The early classical economists simply asserted that this would be the case. They believed in Say's Law, that supply creates its own demand. Say's Law implies that all income generated by the act of supplying output is fully spent on the purchase of that output, so that there is always enough demand. Such a proposition is true of necessity in a barter economy in which there are no non-currently-produced assets. In such circumstances current income can only be used to purchase currently produced output. However, in a monetary exchange economy with non-currently-produced assets, current income need not be used solely to purchase currently produced output. Hence Say's Law is no longer necessarily true but rather it becomes a matter for analysis. Say's Law implies that planned savings must equal planned investment at the level of income generated by the aggregate level of output. Savings represent a leakage of demand in the sense of being that part of current income which households do not use to purchase currently produced output. Investment, on the other hand, represents an injection into demand as firms purchase currently produced capital goods. For Say's Law to hold in the macro exchange economy, an explanation is required for the aggregate equality between the investment plans of firms and the savings plans of households.

According to the early neoclassical theory, sufficient aggregate demand is ensured by interest rate adjustments within the loanable funds market. Investment represents a demand for loanable funds by firms. The demand for loanable funds is inversely related to the rate of interest. As the rate of interest falls, more and more investment projects are likely to yield a rate of return which exceeds the rate of interest, thus increasing the demand for loanable funds by firms. Savings by households, on the other hand, provide the supply of loanable funds. Given the level of income as determined by the supply-side, the level of savings depends on the rate of interest. Households become more willing to forgo present consumption as the rate of interest rises. Hence the level of savings tends to vary directly with the rate of interest. Within the loanable funds market, the rate of interest acts as the allocative mechanism which brings about a market-clearing equilibrium. The rate of interest adjusts to ensure that the level of planned investment equals the level of planned savings, thereby ensuring that there is sufficient aggregate demand to purchase the aggregate supply of output.

The loanable funds market theory was rejected by the Keynesians. They argued that the level of savings does not depend on the rate of interest. Instead, they proposed a consumption function in which the level of consumption (and hence, by implication, the level of savings) depends primarily on the level of income. Furthermore, it is the level of income, not the rate of interest, which adjusts to bring the level of savings into equality with the level of investment. This is the Keynesian multiplier process. If, for example, the level of investment exceeds the level of savings, there is a net injection of demand which leads firms to raise their levels of output and employment, thus generating an increase in income. The increase in income induces a higher level of savings. This expansionary multiplier process continues until a new equilibrium level of income is established at which the level of savings is equal to the level of investment. Likewise the multiplier process can operate in a downward direction leading to a reduction in the level of income if there is a fall in the level of investment.

The crucial question in the Keynesian analysis is the determination of the level of investment. Keynesians argue that even if the level of investment is sensitive to the rate of interest, there is no reason to expect the rate of interest to move in such a way as to generate the level of investment necessary to support the level of income consistent with full employment. This follows from the Keynesian theory of liquidity preference, which locates the determination of the rate of interest in the money market. According to Keynesian theory, interest rate adjustments are the means by which the demand for money is brought into equality with the money supply. The rate of interest does not move to ensure that investment equals savings at the level of income determined by the supply-side. Instead, the level of income and the rate of interest are determined simultaneously on the demand-side. This creates the possibility of demand-side maladjustment in which the equilibrium level of income determined by the demand-side is less than the level of income consistent with full employment. This lack of aggregate demand results in Keynesian involuntary unemployment. Say's Law is seemingly invalidated.

However, this Keynesian analysis of the demand-side is only a partial one. As neoclassical theorists subsequently showed, Keynesian unemployment due to insufficient aggregate demand is a disequilibrium phenomenon. Insufficient aggregate demand is automatically overcome by changes in the general price level. If the equilibrium level of income on the demand-side is less than the full-employment level, the general price level moves downwards, leading to an increase in the real value of the stocks of assets which agents holds. This process, known as the wealth effect, tends to generate an increase in the level of aggregate demand.

The wealth effect operates in two ways. Initially attention focused on the indirect wealth effect, usually known as the Keynes effect. As the general price level falls, this raises the real value of the nominal money supply. This has the effect in the money market of lowering the rate of interest. The fall in the rate of interest tends to stimulate a rise in the level of investment, which in turn sets in motion an expansionary multiplier process. The Keynes effect, however, has no impact on the level of income if investment is insensitive to changes in the rate of interest or if the economy is caught in the so-called liquidity trap, a floor below which the rate of interest is unable to fall. Both these sets of circumstances render the Keynes effect inoperative.

The wealth effect also operates directly, through what is known as the Pigou effect. This is based on the notion that the real value of assets enters as a determinant in the consumption function. Thus a fall in the general price level leads directly to an increase in consumption and, consequently, an increase in aggregate demand even under those circumstances which render the Keynes effect inoperative. Hence adjustments in the general price level, operating through the wealth effect, ultimately ensure that the macro exchange economy generates sufficient aggregate demand to support the full-employment level of output. Say's Law holds.

The Classical Dichotomy

The second fundamental property of the macro exchange economy in equilibrium is the neutrality of money. In the exchange economy money plays the purely passive role of facilitating the exchange process. The quantity of money has no effect on the equilibrium levels of output and employment. In other words, classical theory shows that there is no fundamental difference between a barter exchange economy. C–C, in which real commodities are exchanged directly, and a monetary exchange economy, C–M–C, in which money is the medium of exchange.

Early neoclassical theory considered money solely in its role as a means of exchange, the transactions demand for money. The quantity of money demanded for transactions would vary directly with the nominal value of output. Since the equilibrium level of output is the full-employment level, it follows that in equilibrium the transactions demand for money varies directly with the general price level. Given that the money supply is fixed at a level determined exogenously, market-clearing is achieved in the money market through adjustments in the general price level. The general price level performs the allocative function of bringing the demand for money into equality with the fixed money supply.

This early neoclassical theory of the money market implies that the general price level varies directly with the money supply. This is the quantity theory of money, an age-old idea in economic thought. If, for example, the money supply is increased, agents find themselves with excess money balances, given the nominal value of output. This leads to an increase in the level of aggregate demand. However, since the economy is already at full employment, the only effect of the increase in aggregate demand is a rise in the general price level. This, in turn, raises the transactions demand for money. This process continues until equilibrium is restored in the money market. It follows that, in equilibrium, money is neutral. Money acts as a veil behind which the real sector operates entirely unaffected by its presence. Monetary factors have no influence on the equilibrium levels of real variables such as output and employment. Hence the macro exchange economy is characterized by the so-called Classical Dichotomy. In equilibrium the real sector is independent of the monetary sector. It follows that the classical theory of a micro exchange economy in equilibrium is essentially a real-sector economics.

The Keynesian theory of liquidity preference introduced the demand for money as a store of wealth. Money is one means by which the use of purchasing power may be deferred over time. The asset demand for money depends on the rate of interest, the opportunity cost of holding money. As the rate of interest rises, the asset demand for money falls. The rate of interest moves to ensure market-clearing in the money market, *ceteris paribus*. Thus the general price level is no longer considered to be the sole allocative mechanism in the money market. Furthermore, the general price level is no longer considered to be an allocative mechanism only within the money market. Through the wealth effect, adjustments in the general price level play a key role in ensuring the sufficiency of aggregate demand.

Despite these modifications, money is still neutral. In equilibrium the macro exchange economy is at full employment. The only equilibrium effect of a change in the money supply is a change in the general price level. The neutrality of money is the inevitable implication of the conjunction of a competitive labour market and Say's Law. It is the essential logical truth of monetarism, the modern expression of this fundamental property of the macro exchange economy.

The neutrality of money is, however, a property of a macro exchange economy in equilibrium only. If the real sector is in disequilibrium, money may be non-neutral. For example, if there is insufficient aggregate demand, an increase in the money supply may lead to an increase in the levels of output and employment. But these real effects are only temporary. Once the economy returns to equilibrium, the only impact of the increase in the money supply is a rise in the general price level.

Theories of misallocation

By definition, there are two fundamental requirements for the price mechanism to achieve a perfect allocative equilibrium in an exchange economy. The first fundamental requirement is that the market must have a perfectly atomistic structure. No individual agent or group of agents should have any monopoly power with which to set market price. Agents are, in effect, price-takers. Price is determined solely by the allocative process in accordance with the demand-and-supply theory of price determination. The second fundamental requirement for a perfect allocative equilibrium is that agents must possess perfect (or, at least, sufficient) information. These two fundamental requirements of perfect structure and perfect information represent together the assumption of perfect competition, the ideal case of market conditions.

The information required by agents is of two types. First,

agents must possess all of the information which is necessary to determine their optimal trading plans as the market price varies. This type of information can be called quantity-offer information. Second, agents must possess sufficient information on market conditions in order to make the appropriate price adjustments to achieve market-clearing. This type of information can be called price-adjustment information.

The theoretical problems created by agents having insufficient price-adjustment information are overcome by the traditional Walrasian approach of assuming that a market operates as if it is an auction market with a central auctioneer. The Walrasian auctioneer represents the assumption that all agents have perfect information. Information is costless, obtainable instantaneously at no expense. The auctioneer determines the state of the market and adjusts the market price to achieve a market-clearing equilibrium. The fiction of an auctioneer removes the need to explain the manner in which market forces are translated into the appropriate price adjustments by individual traders.

In the Walrasian approach general equilibrium is achieved through the process of tâtonnement. The auctioneer adjusts prices in all markets simultaneously in response to excess demands and supplies. This process continues until all markets clear. Individual agents are allowed to trade only after the auctioneer has achieved general equilibrium. There is no false trading in the sense of trading at non-market-clearing prices. The restriction that trading only takes place under conditions of general equilibrium removes the problem of how agents react to being unable to fulfill some of their desired trading plans at the prevailing set of prices.

Misallocation occurs if a market fails to reach a perfect allocative equilibrium. There are four basic types of misallocation in a market:

1 The market clears but not at a perfect allocative equilibrium.
2 The market does not clear because the market price is rigid (or slow to adjust).
3 No market-clearing equilibrium exists because either the quantity demanded or supplied is insufficiently sensitive to price.
4 The price-adjustment process is unstable so that there is no convergence to a market-clearing outcome.

Orthodox economic theory has mainly considered the first two types of misallocation: (1) market-clearing at a non-perfect allocative equilibrium; and (2) non-market-clearing due to price rigidity. The special cases of non-existing and unstable equilibria are of peripheral theoretical interest.

What causes misallocation in a market? Orthodox economic theory has located four basic possible causes of misallocation:

1 Non-rational behaviour by agents.
2 Unusual market conditions.

Both of these causes of misallocation lie beyond the scope of orthodox economic theory. They represent *ad hoc* restrictions on the market process, providing a series of special cases to explore. Attention has focused mainly on two other causes of misallocation:

3 Structural imperfections.
4 Informational imperfections.

A market is structurally imperfect if at least one individual agent or group of agents on one side of the market possess sufficient monopoly power with which to influence the market price and the quantity traded simultaneously. The existence of monopoly power results in the quantity traded being less than at the perfect allocative equilibrium under conditions of perfect competition. If the monopoly power is on the demand-side, buyers are able to set the market price more favourably at a level lower than the perfectly competitive level, but with regard to the constraint that the price must be sufficient to ensure that the quantity demanded is actually supplied. Likewise, if the monopoly power is on the supply-side, sellers can set the market price more favourably at a higher level than the perfectly competitive level, again with regard to the constraint of ensuring sufficient demand to purchase the quantity supplied.

For a market to achieve a perfect allocative equilibrium, agents must have sufficient quantity-offer information with which to determine their optimal trading plans and sufficient price-adjustment information with which to achieve the market-clearing price. If agents have imperfect quantity-offer information, the market demand and supply schedules may not coincide with the schedules existing under conditions of perfect information. If agents have imperfect price-adjustment information, the market price may not move towards the market-clearing level.

If all markets within an exchange economy are perfectly competitive and rational agents have sufficient quantity-offer and price-adjustment information, an exchange economy moves to generalized perfect allocative equilibrium. Perfect structure plus perfect information leads to a perfect outcome. It necessarily follows, therefore, that an imperfect outcome must be due to either imperfect structure and/or imperfect information. Hence orthodox economic theory has developed a wide range of imperfectionist theories of misallocation. These imperfectionist theories show how structural and informational imperfections can prevent the attainment of a perfect allocative equilibrium in an exchange economy.

The imperfectionist theories of misallocation can be classified into four basic types depending on whether the cause of misallocation is structural imperfection or informational imperfection, and on whether the market outcome is a market-clearing outcome or a non-market-clearing outcome. This classification is illustrated in table 2.1.

Table 2.1   Imperfectionist theories of misallocation

Types of imperfection	_Types of market outcome_	
	Market-clearing	_Non-market-clearing_
Structural	Type I	Type III
Informational	Type II	Type IV

Type I theories deal with market-clearing outcomes in the presence of structural imperfection. The necessary requirement is the possession of monopoly power by all agents on one side of the market. The result is an imperfectly competitive equilibrium in which both sides of the market are trading the desired quantity at the prevailing market price.

Type II theories deal with market-clearing outcomes in which agents have imperfect information. These theories are concerned with the effects of agents having insufficient quantity-offer information. Agents make their trading plans on the basis of imperfect information. This results in sub-optimal market demand and supply schedules. Hence the market-clearing outcome is not necessarily the outcome which would result under conditions of perfect information.

Type III theories deal with non-market-clearing outcomes caused by structural imperfection. The necessary requirement is the possession of monopoly power by some but not all of the agents on one side of the market. Those agents with no monopoly power whatsoever form a competitive fringe. The agents with monopoly power are able to determine the market price and the quantity traded. The inevitable consequence for the agents forming the competitive fringe is that they are unable to fulfil their desired trading plans at the market price set by the agents with monopoly power. Hence there is non-market-clearing. There is an insider–outsider problem. Those agents who have monopoly power are on the inside with sufficient power to prevent the market price reacting to the allocative pressures exerted by the competitive fringe on the outside.

Type IV theories deal with non-market-clearing outcomes which result from agents having imperfect information. These theories show why price may be rigid (or slow to adjust) in situations of non-market-clearing if agents have insufficient price-adjustment information. The lack of such information may mean that it is optimal for rational agents to leave price unchanged at a non-market-clearing level.

These are the four basic types of imperfectionist theories of misallocation in an exchange economy. Ultimately, in the absence of any *ad hoc* restrictions, orthodox economic theory must explain misallocation by one or more of these four basic types or some combination thereof.

Macro misallocation

Within orthodox economic theory many of the imperfectionist theories of macro misallocation have resulted from the attempt to interpret Keynes's *General Theory*. Keynes claimed that the macro economy may not move automatically to a full-employment equilibrium. Instead, the macro economy may remain for a prolonged period in a position in which the labour market does not clear. If Keynes is interpreted within the classical frame of reference, *The General Theory* becomes a theory of misallocation in the macro exchange economy. The search is on for the orthodox microfoundations which account for Keynesian macro misallocation.

The attempt to interpret Keynes within the classical frame of reference has led to the development of classical Keynesianism. Inevitably, classical Keynesianism has resulted in the elaboration of the macro effects of structural and informational imperfections at the micro level. Classical Keynesianism tries to show in what ways structural and informational imperfections can cause non-market-clearing outcomes.

Initially, Keynesian theory focused on demand-side maladjustment, trying to show that Say's Law is invalid. The central message of early Keynesian theory was that the macro exchange economy may generate insufficient aggregate demand to support a full-employment level of output. However, ultimately it was shown that this required either aggregate demand to be insufficiently sensitive to changes in the general price level or the general price level to be rigid (or slow to adjust). Both of these circumstances were treated as special cases, dependent on *ad hoc* restrictions to the allocative mechanisms operating on the demand-side.

Classical Keynesianism emerged when attention turned to supply-side maladjustment in the labour market. From this perspective, unemployment is seen to occur if the real wage is held at a level above that required for market-clearing in the labour market. The inevitable question which arises is the explanation of why workers would bargain for a money wage which entails that the real wage is too high for the achievement of full employment. Classical theory predicts that, in such circumstances, allocative pressures would ensure lower money wages and hence higher employment levels. The classical Keynesians provided a number of reasons why money wages would tend to be rigid downwards even in the face of substantial unemployment. Workers may be acting irrationally because they suffer from money illusion, bargaining with regard to nominal values rather than real values. Alternatively, the rigidity of money wages may be the result of rational behaviour of workers for whom the relative wage level is the dominant argument in their utility function. Both of these explanations, however, are special cases of peripheral interest.

The downward rigidity of money wages has mainly been explained in terms of structural or informational imperfections in the labour market. The monopoly power of trade unions repre-

sents a structural imperfection in the labour market. Trade unions may be able to use their monopoly power to maintain the
money wage above the market-clearing level. Trade unions, in
effect, use their position to prevent unemployed workers from
bidding wage levels down. The unemployed are not union members, they are outsiders with no direct influence on the wage
bargain between employers and their employees. The institutions
of the labour market render the wage level inoperative as an
allocative mechanism. This is an example of a Type-III imperfectionist theory of misallocation.

The downward rigidity of money wages can also occur because
of informational imperfections. Individual groups of workers may
be unwilling to accept a reduction in their money wage unless all
other groups also accept a similar reduction. Such an assurance
can never be generated by a system of decentralized bargaining.
Without this essential piece of price-adjustment information, no
group of workers is prepared to lead the way. This first-mover
problem is an example of a Type-IV imperfectionist theory of
misallocation.

Classical Keynesian theories of the effects of imperfect information were further developed within the disequilibrium and
neo-Walrasian approaches. In the traditional Walrasian model
the problem of price adjustment is assumed away by the fiction of
a central auctioneer. The neo-Walrasian approach considers the
effects of removing the auctioneer. If there is no auctioneer,
prices may not be set at market-clearing levels. This creates the
possibility of false trading. False trading means that some agents
are unable to fulfil their desired trading plans. In a multi-market
context the failure to fulfil trading plans in one market may have
knock-on effects on the behaviour of agents in other markets,
leading to a position of generalized disequilibrium throughout the
macro exchange economy.

False trading leads to agents being quantity-constrained. The
implications of these quantity constraints have been investigated
by disequilibrium theorists. Agents determine their notional (or
planned) level of purchases simultaneously with their notional
level of sales. If an agent is unable to fulfil the notional sales plan,
an income constraint is placed on the level of purchases which can
be undertaken. The agent must reduce the actual level of purchases below the planned level. For example, if there is excess
supply in the labour market, this leads to a reduction in the level

of effective demand for output by households in the product market. Likewise, if there is excess supply in the product market, this leads to a reduction in the effective demand for labour by firms in the labour market.

The disequilibrium and neo-Walrasian approaches show that, in the absence of price adjustments, the macro exchange economy moves, by a process of quantity adjustment, to a quasi-equilibrium in which there is sufficient effective demand to purchase the actual level of output. The macro exchange economy remains in this position of generalized disequilibrium until the price adjustment process begins to operate.

The removal of the Walrasian auctioneer represents the dropping of the assumption that agents have sufficient price-adjustment information. But, in effect, the neo-Walrasian approach replaces the assumption of perfect information with the new assumption that imperfect information leads to price rigidity. The neo-Walrasian approach offers no explanation as to why this should be the case.

Recent classical Keynesian theory attempts to explain why optimizing agents with imperfect price-adjustment information may find it rational to maintain price at non-market-clearing levels in perfectly competitive markets. In the absence of information about the market-clearing price, agents must form conjectures about the effects of price adjustments. These conjectures may be such that individual agents believe that there is no net gain to be had from adjusting price. Hence a conjectural equilibrium emerges in which price remains at a non-market-clearing level.

Other Keynesian theories have been developed to explain why rational behaviour can lead to price being rigid at non-market-clearing levels. Ultimately these theories always rest on the introduction of some form of structural or informational imperfections. Some of the most recent work by classical Keynesians has tried to move one step further back in the explanation of misallocation by focusing on the underlying causes of structural and informational imperfections. In particular, theories of unemployment have emerged in which the ultimate cause of misallocation is either the existence of increasing returns to scale, the underlying cause of structural imperfection in the product markets, or the existence of transactions costs, one of the underlying causes of informational imperfections. Both of these types of theories are the entirely logical deductions which can be drawn from the imperfectionist theories of classical Keynesianism.

Neoclassical/monetarist theories of misallocation are characterized by the belief that, in the absence of structural imperfections, the price mechanism is able to achieve market-clearing. Neoclassical/monetarist theories of misallocation attempt to explain why imperfect information can lead to sub-optimal market-clearing outcomes. This has lead to the development of the so-called 'new microeconomics', in which agents have imperfect quantity-offer information. The 'new microeconomics' consists of Type-II imperfectionist theories of misallocation.

One effect of agents having imperfect quantity-offer information is that they may not engage in trade until they have acquired sufficient information. This line of argument has been developed in search theory. One application of search theory is the labour supply decision. Households may have imperfect information on the whole set of wage offers. They may quit their current employment in order to engage in search activity to gather the required information. The effect is to reduce the current effective level of labour supply. This leads to the labour market clearing at a level of employment less than the market-clearing level under conditions of perfect information.

Another type of imperfect quantity-offer information occurs if agents have to make offers on the basis of expectations about as yet unknown prices. This raises the possibility that expectations may be mistaken. Hence the price mechanism may achieve a market-clearing outcome for offers which are based on mistaken expectations. For example, the labour supply decision depends on the real wage, but the wage bargain only determines the money wage. In order to determine the real value of the money wage, households require to form expectations about the rate of price inflation during the period for which the wage bargain holds. If the expected inflation rate is greater than the actual rate, the level of labour supply is reduced below the level that would occur under conditions of perfect information. Hence the market-clearing level of employment is reduced.

If there are errors in their expectations, agents may alter their expectations for the next period. Initially, orthodox economic theory modelled this process by using the adaptive-expectations hypothesis, which postulates that the revision of current expectations depends on the errors in past expectations. Adaptive expectations imply that the market outcome adjusts gradually to the perfect allocative equilibrium.

A different perspective on the process of expectation formation is provided by the new classical economics. This orthodox school of thought adopts the rational-expectations hypothesis, which postulates that agents have optimal information on the systematic behaviour of the economy. It follows, therefore, that expectational errors occur only if there is non-systematic behaviour due to external shocks to the economy or surprises in agent behaviour. Thus, according to the new classical economics, sub-optimal market-clearing outcomes are only caused by non-systematic (and, hence, by definition, unknowable) factors. Otherwise the exchange economy is always at a perfect allocative equilibrium.

The main contribution of the new classical economics is to highlight the difference between systematic and non-systematic factors in the quantity-offer information set of agents. The 'new microeconomics' shows that imperfect information on systematic factors leads to the macro exchange economy only gradually adjusting towards a perfect allocative equilibrium over a number of subsequent periods. The new classical economics, on the other hand, deals with the effects of the inevitable lack of information which agents possess about non-systematic factors. The new classical economics shows that these non-systematic factors cause only a temporary (and unavoidable) divergence from a perfect allocative equilibrium to which the macro exchange economy subsequently returns instantaneously.

The limits to classical theory

Classical theory continues to elaborate the properties of the exchange economy with ever-increasing degrees of sophistication. But in so doing classical theory deals only with the allocative mode of activity in which prices and quantities are determined simultaneously. The whole enterprise is founded on the tacit presupposition that there are no limits to the classical frame of reference. Indeed, far from recognizing the limitations to their own approach, classical theorists have begun to turn their attention to explaining aspects of human behaviour previously considered to be non-economic. These followers of classical theory have been described so aptly as the 'social science imperialists'.

The scope and depth of classical theory seems set for further advance.

However, classical theory loses its generality once it is recognized that the notion that economic behaviour falls entirely within the allocative mode of activity is but a highly restrictive presupposition of a purely metaphysical nature. Once this methodological point is taken on board, classical theory is no longer seen as being all-powerful. Limitations are recognized to its relevance with regard to the non-allocative aspects of the capitalist economy. These limitations to the classical frame of reference must be investigated and clearly defined. And new perspectives must be developed to explain non-allocative modes of activity. This is the pluralist method, the very essence of the post-classical approach.

Classical theory interprets a non-perfect allocative equilibrium as misallocation due to the existence of imperfections in the market process. If, however, our presuppositions allow for the possibility of non-allocative modes of activity, this opens up the possibility of alternative theoretical interpretations of economic phenomena. This has the very important practical implication that different theoretical interpretations may generate different policy prescriptions. The possibility of such practical advances, ultimately, is the real justification for introducing new notions of order into economic theory.

3

The Monetary Production Economy

Beyond classical theory

The principal task of this book is to overcome the bounded vision of classical theory by defining the limitations to the relevance of the classical frame of reference. This requires moving beyond that single set of presupposed notions of order. There is a need to develop complementary frames of reference to deal with those aspects of the operation of the capitalist economy which cannot be understood adequately within the classical frame of reference. Classical theory must be recognized as a special theoretical system based on a very restricted view of the nature of order in the economic sphere of human bahaviour. Once this methodological point is accepted, classical theory can be treated no longer as the general theory of economic phenomena.

The classical frame of reference views all economic phenomena as being wholly within the allocative mode of activity. As has been pointed out already, this particular classical frame of reference involves three distinct but inter-related presuppositions: the choice-theoretic, the market-theoretic and the equilibrium-theoretic. The recognition of the possibility of non-allocative modes of activity implies the recognition of the restrictive nature of these classical presuppositions. The three dimensions of the classical frame of reference stand or fall together. A move beyond one necessitates a move beyond all three. The methodological stance adopted here requires just such a move. The classical presuppositions must be seen as giving one conception of economic phenomena. Alternative conceptions based on non-classical presuppositions must also be investigated. Only in this way can economic theory become more general, free of the constraints imposed by any one set of presupposed notions of order.

The present analysis follows one particular path towards a more general conception of economic phenomena. The point of departure is the notion that the monetary context of a capitalist economy significantly affects the nature of behaviour patterns of firms and households. The capitalist economy is characterized by the production of commodities in a monetized economy. The conjunction of these characteristics creates a monetary production economy in which the behaviour patterns of firms and households differ in significant ways from those to be found in an exchange economy. It is this fundamental proposition which opens up the way for a consideration of non-allocative modes of activity.

Classical theory presupposes that all economic activity takes place within the market-theoretic context of behaviour. The market-theoretic presupposition locks classical theory into the allocation–misallocation duality. All observed outcomes fall into one of two mutually exclusive categories of perfect allocative equilibria and non-perfect allocative equilibria, the latter being cases of misallocation caused by the existence of structural and/or informational imperfections. All observed outcomes are either perfect allocative equilibria or cases of misallocation. Classical theory allows for no other type of outcome. This places severe limitations on the type of technological prescriptions which can be provided by economists working within that frame of reference.

The market-theoretic presupposition carries with it the implication that classical theory is the economics of 'real' behaviour. Classical theory is a theory of an exchange economy in which behavior is 'real-focused' in the sense that agents are concerned with the exchange of commodities. In an exchange economy, monetary flows are purely the resultant of the underlying stock-adjustment process. Classical theory adopts a reductionist approach to monetary flows. Monetary flows merely represent 'price × quantity'. They play no active role in determining the position of equilibrium in real terms. Monetary flows are seen to play a significant role only in determining real variables during the process of adjustment when the exchange economy is in disequilibrium. Apart from this, money is not considered to be an essential element in an exchange economy. It is a commodity demanded for transactions and asset purposes. The monetary sector is treated as a separable entity in which an allocative process ensures that the demand for money equals the supply of money.

The belief that money is non-essential is one of the most fundamental limitations which the classical frame of reference imposes on the theoretical conception of economic phenomena. The restrictive nature of the market-theoretic presupposition has to be recognized. But in recognizing the existence of this crucial constraint inherent in orthodox economic thought, it follows that classical theory, as a whole, must be rejected as an adequate theoretical foundation for the study of all aspects of economic phenomena. In a monetary production economy, economic behaviour takes place within a monetary context. The implications of the monetary context of behaviour must be investigated. It is a task to which classical theory has never, indeed could never, address itself. The significance of the monetary context can never be grasped by theorists wedded to the classical presuppositions.

The fundamental proposition of this present analysis is that the monetary context of behaviour leads to non-allocative modes of activity which are qualitatively different from the allocative mode of activity. The move from the classical theory of an exchange economy to the non-classical theory of a monetary production economy entails the rejection of the choice-theoretic presupposition. Classical theory treats all economic behaviour as the result of optimizing choices by rational agents operating within the context of an exchange economy. Rationality is the fundamental law of order within the world of classical theory. Rationality is the single all-embracing principle of economic behaviour. From the perspective of classical theory, non-rational behaviour is, by definition, non-economic behaviour.

An alternative perspective to the choice-theoretic presupposition is provided by the behavioural approach. In the behavioural approach, firms and households are not treated as rational agents able to use their available information sets so as to optimize with respect to well-defined goals. Rather, firms and households are viewed as adopting decision rules which are considered to be appropriate in the circumstances, but such rules may be revised in the light of past experience or the acquisition of new information. The context of behaviour will play a crucial role in determining the decision rules used by firms and households. The behavioural approach therefore allows for the possibility that the monetary context can have a significant effect on behaviour. Thus the adoption of the behavioural approach is a necessary element, albeit an implicit one, in the development of the theory of a monetary production economy.

The adoption of this alternative approach implies a method of analysis in which all theoretical models must be constructed using behavioural assumptions which are an acceptable realistic approximation to the observed behaviour patterns under investigation. Given realistic assumptions about observed behaviour patterns, the theoretical economist may pursue two different types of question. The first type of question is to ask why particular agents adopt particular behaviour patterns under specific circumstances. This backward-looking question takes the economist into the realms of psychology and organization theory, subject fields with much to say on the decision-making processes of individuals and organizations. There should be no reductionist presumption that all observed behaviour can be ultimately explained in terms of some single, all-embracing principle. The second theoretical question pursued within the behavioural approach is the forward-looking question as to the implications of the observed behaviour patterns. This involves deducing the aggregate outcome implied by the behaviour patterns of individual agents. The results of this type of theoretical analysis provide the means with which to deduce the technological prescriptions sought by applied economists. But in adopting the behavioural approach, it must always be remembered that theoretical models and their implied technological prescriptions are applicable only if the underlying assumptions remain realistic. Theoretical models should not be treated as a source of laws of general applicability. Too often the axiomatic status accorded to the assumption of rationality has blinded economists to the empirical limitations of their models. Those who follow the behavioural approach should have no such delusions about the status of their models.

The behavioural approach offers an alternative method of analysis to the choice-theoretic approach of classical theory. In particular, the behavioural approach rejects the instrumentalist method used to justify the continued acceptance by classical theory of the axiom of rationality, clearly an unrealistic assumption. The instrumentalist method adopts the position that the realism of assumptions is not a relevant criterion on which to base the selection of theories. According to the instrumentalist method, theoretical models should be judged primarily on the grounds of their predictive power. This methodological stance is very dangerous. In denying the relevance of realistic assumptions, instrumentalism rejects the pursuit of explanation as an objective. Explanation must, by definition, involve trying to justify observed relationships in terms of realistic assumptions. Instrumentalism replaces the pursuit of explanation with the pursuit of correlation. This results in statistical associations which are unexplained except in terms of the assumptions from which they have been generated. If these assumptions are not based on observed reality, the explanations are meaningless as are any implied technological prescriptions. The instrumentalist method has the effect of rendering the underlying presuppositions of any theoretical system immune from scrutiny. Such scrutiny is deemed irrelevant in the eyes of an instrumentalist. It is only the predictive power of a model which should be subject to examination.

The instrumentalist justification for the use of the axiom of rationality has not only blinded the followers of classical theory to the irrelevance of their models for the analysis of non-allocative behaviour. The theoretical limitations of the choice-theoretic approach within the classical frame of reference have also been ignored. The use of the axiom of rationality means that determinate theoretical models can be constructed. Rational agents with perfect information make the optimal choice in any particular choice situation. However, once the more general and more realistic assumption is made that agents may have an information set of varying degrees of completeness, it is no longer possible to construct unique determinate models. There is an infinite variety of assumptions which can be made on the nature of informational imperfections and the learning procedures which agents adopt in such circumstances. The choice-theoretic presupposition breaks down entirely.

Imperfect information also raises severe difficulties for the equilibrium-theoretic presupposition of classical theory. Under conditions of imperfect information, agents are likely to adopt various learning procedures. This creates a disequilibrium adjustment process, but the nature of the adjustment process will depend on the particular informational imperfections present and the particular learning procedures adopted. It follows, therefore, that there is no reason whatsoever why the adjustment process should converge on the equilibrium outcome associated with conditions of perfect information. The classical Keynesian theories of conjectural equilibrium are one example of an adjustment process, under conditions of imperfect information, which does not result in a perfect allocative equilibrium. The inevitable conclusion to be drawn is that imperfect information represents a theoretical 'black hole' for classical theory.

The problem of imperfect information demands the adoption of the behavioural approach. Theoretical analysis must start from realistic assumptions about information sets and learning procedures. This may involve empirical observation and the use of the findings of related subject fields such as psychology. Not surprisingly, the revolutionary implications for analytical methods have been resisted by the majority of the economics profession. The followers of classical theory have attempted to accommodate the implications of imperfect information within the classical set of presupposed notions of order. Examples of this accommodation are the whole series of expectational hypotheses which imply that agents adapt their expectations in a fixed, mechanistic manner. These adaptive-expectations hypotheses are too simple and rigid to provide a realistic approximation to the complex learning procedures used by individuals and organizations. But at least, to their credit, the adaptive-expectations hypotheses point in the right direction by accepting that agents do adapt their behaviour through learning. More recently, however, the limitations of the adaptive-expectations hypotheses have led the followers of classical theory to adopt the rational-expectations hypothesis, in which agents are assumed to have complete information on the systematic element of economic phenomena. In other words, the rational-expectations hypothesis assumes that agents know all that can be conceivably known. Agents with rational expectations have no need to learn. The rational-expectations hypothesis is but the most recent example of the tendency to retain the classical assumption of perfect information, albeit in evermore sophisticated guises. Another 'escape' from the implications of imperfect information is to postulate that agents have complete probabilistic knowledge in the sense of being able to attach a probability to all possible outcomes. This allows agents to make rational choices based on the optimization of expected values. In other words, agents are assumed to face situations of risk rather than uncertainty. This is the approach which underlies the search theories of misallocation developed within the 'new microeconomics'. It is yet another attempt to deal with imperfect information within the classical frame of reference and as such is doomed to' be inadequate when judged from outside the classical presuppositions. It is yet another example of the bounded vision which pervades modern economic theory. Imperfect information requires the development of new notions of order and new methods of analysis – that is, a move beyond the confines of classical theory.

The present analysis offers one way forward beyond the confines of classical theory. The starting-point is the theory of a monetary production economy as inspired by Keynes in his *General Theory*. That work has acted as a catalyst for the intuitive insights to which this present analysis seeks to give form. Keynes can be seen as having adopted the behavioural approach. He started with a series of simple but realistic assumptions about the observed patterns of behaviour in a monetary production economy. From these assumptions the properties which would be exhibited by a monetary production economy were deduced.

In this chapter the nature of a monetary production economy is examined. This involves drawing heavily on the basic insights contained within *The General Theory*. But it is important to remember that the validity or otherwise of this implied interpretation of Keynes is not the issue. Such questions of interpretation are doctrinal matters which are the proper province of historians of economic thought. They are not the concern of the present analysis. This is not to deny the importance of these questions but, rather, to prevent unhelpful side-tracking. The point at issue is whether or not the monetary production economy is a theoretical construct which can provide useful insights into the operation of the capitalist economy.

The significance of the monetary context is that firms and households adopt patterns of behaviour in which they seek to meet objectives with respect to monetary flows. Behaviour in a monetary production economy is flow-determined, not stock-determined. Monetary flows are not the result of a stock-adjustment process but a key determinant of the behaviour of firms and households. The monetary production economy is characterized by non-allocative modes of activity in which the monetary flows are an integral part. The nature of money cannot be understood in terms of some separate monetary sector. The whole of a monetary production economy is a monetary sector.

In a monetary production economy, firms undertake production in order to generate a monetary revenue inflow in excess of the incurred monetary cost outflow. The difference between the revenue inflow and cost outflow is monetary profit, the principal *raison d'être* of capitalist firms. The context of firm behaviour can be characterized as M–C–M. Monetary flows are the central concern for firms, not the trading of physical goods and services. Firms trade physical inputs and outputs in order to achieve monetary objectives. Firms operate in a sequential manner, with monetary flows being of primary importance. The significance of this observation is overlooked by classical theory, which attaches only a secondary importance to monetary flows, treating them as being entirely consequent on the underlying stock-adjustment process. From this perspective, money is but a veil behind which real economic processes operate entirely unaffected by its presence.

The behaviour of households, is also affected by this monetary context. Households make their decisions on the level of their monetary outflows on consumption and savings with respect to the level of their monetary inflow of income received from the production process. It is this observation which Keynes enshrined in his notion of the consumption function. It is entirely inappropriate to liken the sequential decision process within households to a barter stock-adjustment process in which households exchange their stocks of factors of production directly for stocks of consumer goods and services.

Monetary flows are, by definition, equal to 'price × quantity'. But it does not follow from this that prices and quantities must necessarily be determined simultaneously in the manner suggested by the demand-and-supply theory of price determination. This occurs only in the very special circumstances in which agents are operating within the allocative mode of activity. In general, however, prices and quantities are determined independently by very different behavioural processes. It is a fundamental property of a monetary production economy that prices and quantities are determined quite separately. The classical presuppositions have led orthodox economists into believing, quite mistakenly, that the special case holds in general.

Output and employment in a monetary production economy

The output decision
Capitalist firms seek a number of, sometimes conflicting, goals.

Principal among these goals is the pursuit of monetary profits. Firms seek to earn profits by the production and marketing of goods and services. The marketing activities of a firm are those associated with generating a demand for its output. The production process, on the other hand, is concerned with supplying the output required to meet the demand generated. It follows, therefore, that firms necessarily display a sequential behaviour pattern in which marketing activities are of primary importance, with the production process having only a secondary, indeed almost residual, role.

The sequential nature of the decision process within firms is enshrined in the output decision. The output decision is the fundamental behaviour pattern of firms in a monetary production economy. Firms set their output levels with respect to their expectations of the level of demand for their output. It is this single behaviour pattern which ultimately gives a monetary production economy its fundamental property of being a demand-side economy. In a monetary production economy, demand determines supply.

The expectations which affect the output decision are what Keynes designated short-term expectations. It is a convenient simplifying-assumption that these expectations are correct since the effect of mistaken short-term expectations is only to create temporary variations in output and stock-building as firms seek, by a process of trial and error, to discover the actual level of demand.

The demand for any product of a firm depends on three separate elements:

1 An individual product's share of the total demand for the particular product group within which any individual product is located.
2 The share of the particular product group in the aggregate demand for all goods and services produced in the economy.
3 The level of aggregate demand.

Since the central concern of the present analysis is with the short-run behaviour of the macro economy, it is the level of aggregate demand which is of primary importance. The distribution of aggregate demand between and within product groups may have consequences for the aggregate level of employment if firms and/or product groups vary in their propensities to employ and to lay-off. In the short-run, however, it seems valid to suppose that such influences are normally relatively unimportant at the aggregate level. Hence it is assumed that the distribution of aggregate demand is fixed. It is beyond the scope of the present study to provide an adequate theory dealing with the competitive and structural factors which determine the distribution of the aggregate demand. Thus, for present purposes, it is assumed that firms set the level of output solely with respect to their (correct) short-term expectations on the level of aggregate demand. This is the assumption which Keynes adopted in *The General Theory*.

It follows, therefore, from the nature of the output decision of individual firms, that for the economy as a whole, aggregate output depends on aggregate demand. As the level of aggregate demand changes, the level of aggregate output will tend to move in the same direction. But this behavioural relationship entails a link between two very different spheres of activity. Aggregate demand is a monetary flow whereas aggregate output is a real flow of goods and services. There is a gap between these two spheres of activity, a gap which firms must bridge in the output decision. Firms hold (short-term) expectations on product demand in real terms which must be based on their expectations of the monetary value of aggregate demand. This is a unique, but very significant, feature of a monetary production economy.

The gap between aggregate demand and the aggregate supply of output by firms means that there is no one-to-one relationship between aggregate demand and aggregate supply. Firms can respond to (expected) changes in aggregate demand in three different ways:

1 By changing the level of output.
2 By changing price.
3 By rescheduling through time by inventories or customer queuing.

Firms may respond in any one of these ways or by some combination of them. It follows, therefore, that the output decision is a complex one. There is no simple single rule-of-thumb at work. There is no fixed propensity to supply with respect to changes in the level of aggregate demand. The propensity to supply varies with circumstances.

It seems plausible, however, that the following behaviour

patterns are likely to be exhibited by firms. If firms hold short-term expectations of only a temporary rise in aggregate demand, and if, furthermore, firms are currently operating under conditions of relatively full utilization of their existing capacity, it follows that firms are more likely to respond by raising prices and building-up customer queues, rather than by increasing the level of output. On the other hand, firms are more likely to increase their level of output if they expect a more permanent rise in aggregate demand under conditions of relative under utilization of capacity.

If firms expect a fall in aggregate demand, firms are more likely to react by cutting price and stock-building if the fall in demand is expected to be only temporary and if firms are operating near to their minimum-acceptable level of capacity utilization. Firms are more likely to respond by reducing output if the change in demand is expected to be more permanent and if there is relatively full-capacity utilization.

Thus, to reiterate, in a monetary production economy, the aggregate level of output is primarily determined by the level of aggregate demand. But there is no fixed propensity to supply with respect to changes in the level of aggregate demand. The propensity to supply will vary with circumstances. The propensity to supply will tend to depend principally on: (1) the direction of the change in aggregate demand; (2) the rate of the change in aggregate demand; (3) the expected degree of permanence of the change in aggregate demand; and (4) the current level of capacity utilization.

The employment decision

As an initial simplification, the employment decision of firms can be portrayed as following on directly from the output decision. Given the level of output, the required level of employment is uniquely determined by the technical conditions of production. It follows, therefore, that the aggregate level of employment depends on the level of aggregate demand. Thus the direction of causality runs from the demand side to the supply side. This is an essential, and indeed the most significant, characteristic of a monetary production economy.

Although this initial simplified view of the employment decision contains the essential nature of the behaviour patterns at work, it is an inadequate representation of the complexities involved in the employment decision. It glosses over those factors which may be of great significance in the formulation of appropriate employment-generating policies.

An important complication with the employment decision is the recognition that the propensity to employ with respect to changes in the level of output is not uniform across all types of labour. The initial simplification deals only with labour whose employment is directly related to the level of production activities within the firm. However, in modern firms, a substantial proportion of the workforce is employed in administrative and marketing activities. The propensity to employ labour within these activities as the level of output changes is relatively low in comparison with the propensity to employ within the production activities of the firm. At least this would appear to be a realistic assumption, even though long-term trends in technological change may bring about a convergence between these employment propensities, particularly through a lowering of the employment propensities of production-related occupations.

The propensity to employ within any particular activity will tend to vary with the type of skill involved. There is an important distinction between, on the one hand, workers with general skills of which there is relatively little shortage and, on the other, workers with firm-specific skills in whom firms must invest substantially in training costs or workers with general skills which are in short supply. These latter categories of workers will tend to be less prone to lay-offs and redundancy than workers with more easily available general skills.

Thus, within the workforce there is a spectrum of employment propensities. At one end of the spectrum there are those workers who are treated as highly variable factors of production with relatively high employment (and lay-off) propensities with respect to changes in output. At the other end of the spectrum there are those workers who are treated as almost quasi-fixed factors with relatively low employment propensities with respect to changes in output.

Just as with the overall propensity to supply, the overall propensity to employ will vary with circumstances. The four main determinants of the overall propensity to employ are: (1) the direction of the change in the level of output; (2) the rate of the change in the level of output; (3) the expected degree of permanence in the change in the level of output; and (4) the current rate of labour utilization. The propensity to employ is likely to be greater as output levels increase than the propensity to lay-off as output levels fall. This asymmetry reflects the desire of firms to avoid, at least initially, having to lay off the more quasi-fixed elements in their workforce. However, the greater the size and the expected permanence of any fall in output levels, the more likely is the propensity to lay-off to rise. Finally, the propensity to employ is likely to rise as the rate of labour utilization rises since it is less likely that the existing labour force will be able to cope with the higher output levels.

The employment decision and the output decision tend to be interactive. For example, circumstances may arise, such as shortages of skilled labour, in which the propensity to employ is insufficient to provide for planned expansion in output. This employment constraint will lead to a fall in the propensity to supply, so that firms will tend to respond to an expected increase in aggregate demand by increasing price and customer queues to a greater extent than otherwise.

Aggregate demand

In a monetary production economy the levels of output and employment depend primarily on the level of aggregate demand. The crucial question becomes the analysis of the processes by which the level of aggregate demand is itself determined. The analysis of the determination of the level of aggregate demand in a monetary production economy is Keynes's key contribution in *The General Theory*.

Keynes distinguished two components of aggregate demand: consumption and investment. Consumption is the monetary flow of expenditure from households used to purchase the final consumer products of firms. Investment is the monetary flow of expenditure from firms to other firms in exchange for capital goods such as plant and machinery. Together consumption and investment comprise the monetary flow of aggregate demand within a monetary production economy. In *The General Theory* Keynes outlined the determinants of the consumption and investment decisions. Keynes's empirical hypotheses on these two decisions still remain valid as characterizations of their essential nature.

The consumption decision

Perhaps the most far-reaching of all Keynes's insights is his representation of the consumption decision by households. The Keynesian consumption function is based on the empirical hypothesis that households determine their current monetary outflow of expenditure on consumer goods and services with respect to their current monetary inflow of income. The rate of the consumption expenditure flow is primarily flow-determined. The rate of the monetary flow of consumption expenditure depends on the rate of the aggregate monetary flow.

Keynes also recognized that the propensity to consume with respect to money income is less than unity. Thus, as the rate of the monetary income flow rises, the rate of the consumption expenditure flow rises but by less than the rise in the rate of the income flow. In other words, the rate of monetary outflow on savings by households varies directly with the rate of monetary inflow of income. Hence the Keynesian consumption function is based on the empirical hypothesis that households determine the allocation of their monetary outflow between consumption and savings with respect to the rate of monetary inflow of income. It is this behaviour pattern which underpins the Keynesian multiplier process.

Classical theory, while not denying the dependency of savings on the level of income, does tend to obscure the significance of this dependency. Classical theory pushes the savings–income relationship into the background, treating income as the budget constraint within which allocative decisions need to be taken. Furthermore, classical theory allows one and only one level of income in equilibrium, namely the full-employment level of income. Classical theory views the savings decision as an allocative decision in which households must allocate their current income between the competing alternatives of consumption and savings. The relevant price in this allocative process is the rate of interest.

Keynes saw, very perceptively, that the household's decision on the distribution of its income between consumption and savings does not fall within the allocative mode of activity. The level of savings does not depend on the rate of interest. Rather the consumption–savings decision is an example of the utilization mode of activity. In the utilization mode of activity, the rate of utilization depends on the rate of the relevant monetary flow. The consumption–savings decision is an example of this mode of activity. The rate of utilization of the income flow as a consumption expenditure flow depends on the rate of the income flow. This is a very different mode of activity from the allocative mode in which decisions are characterized as depending on the relevant price variable. Classical theory fails to distinguish the utilization mode of activity as a mode of activity which is qualitatively different from the allocative mode of activity. This failure stems from its reductionist approach which assumes away the significance of the monetary context in affecting behaviour patterns.

Although consumption (and savings) are primarily determined by money income, there are a number of secondary factors which may be of significance in certain circumstances. The most important of these secondary factors is likely to be the wealth position of households. Households are able to finance current consumption by means other than current income. Households may be able to liquidate part of their accumulated stock of assets or, alternatively, they may undertake debt-financed consumption by borrowing from the financial sector. The level of debt-financed consumption is likely to be closely related to the level of income, inasmuch as financial institutions use the current income of borrowers to determine the level of credit facilities they are prepared to extend. None the less, the level of asset holding is likely to enter the consumption–savings decision as a factor which is independent of current income. Thus the level of current consumption is partly stock-determined.

The recognition of the influence of the wealth stock on the level of current consumption opens up the possibility of a wealth effect as the real value of the wealth stock changes. The real value of the wealth stock depends on the nominal value of the wealth stock relative to the aggregate price level. If either of these components changes, the real value of the wealth stock is changed, and this may have an effect on the level of consumption.

Classical theory has tended to view the wealth effect as one of the principal allocative mechanisms for ensuring the sufficiency of aggregate demand in an exchange economy. For example, if the macro exchange economy is in a position of disequilibrium with insufficient aggregate demand to maintain full employment, classical theory argues that the lack of aggregate demand in the product market will produce a fall in the price level, which will in turn raise the real value of the wealth stock and thereby generate a positive wealth effect that stimulates the level of aggregate demand. This is a far too restrictive and optimistic view of the wealth effect, as many have realized. A number of influences are likely to affect the strength and direction of the wealth effect, including the ultimate source of the change in the real value of wealth, the size of the change and the expectations about future changes, to name but three of the more significant influences. Above all, the classical presumption of a favourable wealth effect is challenged most fundamentally by the recognition that the wealth stock overwhelmingly consists of assets held by some agents but representing the debts of other agents. The classical notion of a wealth effect operating on a net wealth base sweeps the problem under the proverbial carpet, assuming as it does that creditors and debtors react in equal but opposite ways to any given change in their real position. Such an assumption is unlikely to be empirically realistic. Debtors, almost by definition, are likely to have a higher propensity to spend than creditors. Under these circumstances, a fall in the aggregate price level will tend to produce a decrease in aggregate demand, not the increase suggested by classical theory. The implication of this is that far from being the allocative mechanism presumed by classical theory, the wealth effect can create an unstable adjustment process, producing a cumulative divergence away from the full-employment equilibrium. In the light of these remarks, it is indeed surprising that classical theory should put so much weight on the role of the wealth effect as one of the key automatic self-adjustment mechanisms in an exchange economy. A house built on sand if ever there was one.

The investment decision

The other main component of aggregate demand is investment, the purchase of capital goods by firms. In analysing the investment decision of firms, it is necessary to distinguish between those factors affecting the potential propensity to invest and those affecting the actual propensity to invest. The potential propensity to invest represents the desired changes which firms wish to make to their existing capital stock. It sets some notional limit on the investment projects which firms may be willing to undertake. The actual propensity to invest represents those potential investment projects which are actually undertaken during a particular time period. The degree to which potential investment is actualized will tend to vary significantly over time.

There are four principal reasons why firms may desire changes in their existing capital stock: (1) capacity expansion; (2) replacement; (3) diversification; and (4) technique substitution. Firms undertake investment for capacity expansion purposes when they find that their existing capital stock is insufficient to support the desired level of output. Faced with a capacity constraint, firms seek to invest in additional capacity, provided the higher level of output is expected to be the normal state of affairs. Temporary peaks in the level of output can be met by above-normal utilization of the existing capacity. Alternatively, they can be met by some form of customer rationing, either through higher price or over time by lengthening queues.

Replacement investment is required when the existing capital stock physically depreciates to such an extent that it requires to be replaced by a new capital stock. The physical depreciation of capital tends to raise the costs of production through increased frequency of breakdown, repair and servicing. Eventually this depreciation may raise the costs of production above the maximum acceptable level, at which point replacement is unavoidable. However, until that critical point is reached, firms have the option to defer replacement investment, thus extending the life of the existing capital stock beyond that which would be normally expected. The level of replacement investment potentially required at any point in time depends on the time profile of past investments. This creates the potential for a self-perpetuating cyclical pattern in investment in which periods of high, then low, rates of investment will subsequently generate periods of high, then low, rates of replacement investment.

Firms who seek to diversify into new product areas, may require to invest if their existing capital stock cannot be used for the production of these new products. Investment is not a necessary consequence in such circumstances since firms may enter the new product areas by means of the acquisition route. Thus the level of diversification investment depends on two sets of factors. First, there are those factors which affect the overall level of diversification activity, such as the rate of technological progress, the stage of the product life-cycle and the whole array of other competitive pressures which push firms to seek growth in new product areas. Second, there is the group of factors which determine the distribution of diversification activity between diversification involving investment in new capacity and other forms of diversification such as entry by acquisition and concentric diversification using existing production processes.

The final type of investment is that associated with technique substitution. Firms may wish to change the techniques of production used for their existing product in favour of more cost-effective techniques. This occurs if technological progress or a change in factor prices leads to the costs of production of the current techniques being in excess of some acceptable maximum level. It is this type of investment, regulated as it is by the price mechanism, which has been given prominence by classical theory. Firms are expected to invest in those techniques which use relatively intensively, the relatively cheap and abundant factor. However, it is unlikely that technique substitution is a primary reason for investment in its own right, except in the case of very significant changes in technology or factor prices. Normally, technique substitution takes place through investment for reasons of capacity expansion, replacement or diversification. As firms undertake investment for these purposes, then and only then are firms likely to consider the range of techniques available.

Thus, overall, the potential level of investment is affected by a number of factors, prominent among which are the level of activity, the time profile of past investment, the rate of technological change, competitive pressures and changes in factor prices. It is therefore difficult to make any broad generalizations about the determination of the potential level of investment. However, inasmuch as capacity expansion is likely to be a significant reason for investment, the potential level of investment is likely to fluctuate in line with the level of activity in the economy. This creates the possibility of a virtuous circle in which a high level of activity tends to stimulate the potential level of investment which, if actualized, will provide a further stimulus to the level of activity. Naturally this process of cumulative causation can operate in reverse, creating a vicious circle in which low levels of activity and investment are mutually self-reinforcing.

Having considered the determinants of the potential level of investment, the question arises: what determines the degree to which the potential propensity to invest is actualized? The actual propensity to invest is likely to depend on two sets of factors: (1) those affecting the ability of firms to finance potential investment projects; and (2) those affecting the willingness of firms to undertake financially-feasible investment projects.

There are two principal sources of finance with which firms can fund investment projects. Firms can finance investment projects internally, by drawing on accumulated holdings of retained earnings, or externally, by borrowing. The availability of internal finance depends on the profit performance of the firm. In any period total profits earned depend on the profit margin per unit of output and the level of output. The profit margin is likely to depend largely on the degree of competitive pressures which firms face. These pressures are likely to increase when there are low levels of activity. It is precisely in these circumstances that firms are likely to face upward pressure on their average costs of production, resulting from the loss of economies of scale. Firms operating at low levels of output find that each unit of output must carry a higher burden of fixed costs. But the increase in competitive pressures means that firms are less able to pass on the higher average costs in the form of higher prices. The overall result is likely to be a fall in profits. It follows therefore that there is a tendency for the ability of firms to fund investment internally to be directly related to the level of activity. As the level of activity rises, profits increase, providing firms with the source of funding for their potential investment projects. This positive two-way interaction between profits and the level of activity can operate in both an expansionary and a contractionary direction and creates and possibility of upswings and downswings in the behaviour of the macro economy.

The second source of funding for investment is borrowing. The ability of firms to borrow through the provision of credit facilities by the banking system is normally entirely demand-determined, provided firms are rated as secure. Firms only face borrowing restrictions if there is a credit squeeze. Under these circumstances firms may find credit rationed through restrictions in the amount available and its timing, and also through higher rates of interest. Firms are also able to borrow through the sale of debt instruments in the financial markets. Such instruments require to be priced competitively in relation to other substitute forms for holding wealth. Firms can also obtain finance externally by issuing new equity, rather than borrowing. Again the viability of this means of raising finance depends crucially on current market conditions in the financial sector.

Overall, it is likely that firms normally face no effective constraints as regards either the availability of potential investment projects or the availability of finance, although both are likely to increase with the level of activity. Hence it follows that the critical element in the investment decision are those factors which influence the willingness of firms to use their available funds to finance potential investment projects. Traditionally, economic theory has focused attention on the rate of interest as the principal determinant of the willingness to invest. The rate of interest represents the cost of borrowing as well as the opportunity cost for retained earnings used for investment purposes. Classical theory sees the rate of interest as the price mechanism which regulates the loanable funds market, ensuring that there is equality between the demand for loanable funds by firms for investment purposes and the supply of loanable funds.

Both classical theory and Keynes portrayed firms as estimating the expected rate of return from potential investment projects. Keynes referred to this expected rate of return as the marginal efficiency of capital. It is based on the net monetary revenue inflows which firms expect to be generated from the monetary cost outflows incurred by the investment project. The marginal efficiency of capital is an entirely *ex ante* concept, a calculation by firms on the basis of expected monetary flows. Firms are only willing to undertake those potential investment projects in which the marginal efficiency of capital exceeds the rate of interest.

The marginal efficiency of capital represents a particular pattern of behaviour. It has no connection whatsoever with the famous capital controversy in economic theory over the theoretical problems associated with the concept of aggregate capital. Yet many have claimed such a connection, viewing Keynes's concept of the marginal efficiency of capital as being identical with the classical concept of the marginal product of capital. Those who adopt this interpretation of Keynes, have failed to recognize that Keynes's concept of the marginal efficiency of capital is beyond the classical frame of reference. The marginal efficiency of capital relates to calculations about expected monetary flows. It does not involve any notion of aggregate capital. It refers to a behaviour pattern outside of the allocative mode of activity. The marginal efficiency of capital relates to behaviour within the context of a monetary production economy. It is certainly a concept which has classical origins and, in this respect, it is misleading and a source of confusion. But, despite its classical origins, Keynes clearly interpreted the marginal efficiency of capital in a non-classical manner, a concept with a valid meaning only in terms of the rules and grammar of Keynes's non-classical language-game.

By focusing on the rate of interest, classical theory has tended to overemphasize its importance. The rate of interest is only likely to have a significant impact on the investment decision once it reaches some critical level, at which point it becomes a powerful disincentive effect. It does not follow from this observation, however, that reducing the rate of interest leads to a direct stimulus to the level of investment. Low rates of interest are a facilitating factor in the willingness of firms to invest, possibly even a necessary condition. But low rates of interest, on their own, are insufficient.

The secondary role assigned to the rate of interest follows from the fact that the investment decision is, fundamentally, dependent on the confidence of firms in the future. This is what Keynes called the state of long-term expectations. The investment decision is, inevitably, plagued by uncertainty. The returns from an investment project accrue over a period of years. Firms will only invest if they have sufficient confidence that the future will allow the realization of the expected returns from investment. As Keynes rightly understood, the mathematical calculations on the expected rate of return are, ultimately, grounded on beliefs about the future which cannot themselves be evaluated in any objective manner. Human decision-makers can never know what the future holds. This uncertainty cannot be overcome by creating probability distributions. Indeed, this simple fact of life is one of the key insights contained in Keynes's *General Theory*. Without confidence there can be no investment. This is why the rate of interest is relatively insignificant. It is entirely overshadowed by the state of long-term expectations. Lowering the rate of interest is unlikely, on its own, to be sufficient to bring about a significant change in long-term expectations. A much more important influence on the state of long-term expectation is the experience of firms in the recent past. Firms are likely to be more confident about the future in circumstances where there has been a recent increase in the level of activity of a sustained nature. The experience of growing levels of aggregate demand leads to expectations of future growth. This reflects the very powerful human belief in continuity.

It follows from this discussion on the nature of the investment decision that investment, like consumption, is likely to be primarily flow-determined. Inasmuch as changes in the rate of monetary flow reflect changes in the level of output, this is likely to lead to increases in the number of potential investment projects (particularly for reasons of capacity expansion) as well as to increases in the ability to finance these projects (through higher profits) and to a greater willingness to undertake these projects (as the level of business confidence improves).

The multiplier process

It follows from the nature of the consumption and investment decisions that the level of aggregate demand in a monetary production economy is primarily flow-determined. The level of aggregate demand depends on the rate of the monetary income flow. This has a fundamental consequence of great significance, namely that changes in the rate of the monetary flow is the mechanism which regulates the level of aggregate demand in a monetary production economy. The rate of the monetary flow adjusts to ensure that planned investment equals planned savings. This adjustment process is the Keynesian multiplier process. It is the crucial feature of a monetary production economy, implied by the behaviour patterns of households and firms. It is the recognition of the role of the multiplier process in a monetary production economy which remains one of the central contributions of Keynes's *General Theory*.

The multiplier adjustment process arises from the circular flow of monetary income, which constitutes the context of behaviour within a monetary production economy. The flow of monetary expenditure from households (on consumption) and firms (on investment) provides the revenue inflow for firms, generating, in turn, the flow of monetary income to households. This circular flow is in balance when investment equals savings. Savings is that part of the monetary inflow which households do not use for expenditure. Savings represents a leakage from the circular flow, that part of the monetary flow which does not become a revenue inflow to firms. Investment, on the other hand, is an injection into the circular flow, an additional source of revenue inflow to firms as a whole. If the level of investment expenditure matches the level of savings, the circular flow of income is in balance. The rate of flow of monetary expenditure equals the rate of flow of monetary income.

If there is an autonomous, non-flow-generated, change in the rate of the monetary expenditure flow, the rate of the monetary income flow adjusts until investment and savings are brought into balance. For example, suppose there is an improvement in the state of long-term expectations due to some exogenous influence. This leads to a rise in the rate of flow of monetary expenditure on investment which means a rise in the rate of the monetary income flow. This leads, in turn, to further rises in the rate of the monetary expenditure flow as households increase their consumption expenditure and firms may further increase their investment expenditure. This generates further rises in the rate of the monetary income flow and further subsequent rises in the rate of the monetary expenditure flow, and so on. The rises in the rate of the monetary income flow also lead to increases in the rate of the savings flow since the propensity to consume of households is less than unity. The expansionary process continues until the rate of the savings flow equals the new higher rate of the investment expenditure flow. If the process is stable, a new dynamic equilibrium is established with the rates of flow of monetary expenditure and income once again being equal.

The multiplier process is one of cumulative causation, an essential characteristic of a monetary production economy. Once a monetary production economy begins to move in one direction, it automatically generates a self-perpetuating momentum which maintains the direction of change. Thus a rise in expenditure generates further rises in expenditure. The economy becomes locked into a virtuous circle of expansion. Equally, a fall in expenditure generates a vicious circle of decline. This multiplier effect is entirely due to the nature of the consumption and investment decisions. The potentially explosive nature of the process arises from the accelerator effect of flow-determined investment. If it is only consumption which is flow-determined, a propensity to consume less than unity implies a stable process which tends towards a dynamic equilibrium. The effect of investment also being flow-determined is to create the possibility of an overall propensity to spend with respect to monetary income greater than unity.

Demand-side economics

Within a monetary production economy, it is the demand side which is the driving force. The level of aggregate demand determines the levels of output and employment. This is a complete reversal of the causal sequence to be found in an exchange economy. In an exchange economy it is the supply side which is the driving force. The supply side sets the equilibrium levels of output and employment, with the price mechanisms on the demand side ensuring the sufficiency of aggregate demand.

In a monetary production economy, Say's Law is not a fundamental property of the macro economy. Supply does not create its own demand. Quite the reverse occurs. Demand creates its own supply. This creates the possibility that a monetary production economy may stabilize at a dynamic equilibrium in which the actual levels of output and employment are less than the potential levels. It is a key feature of a monetary production economy that the rate of monetary flow may adjust to bring the rates of flow of investment and savings into equality but at a level of aggregate demand which is insufficient to support the full employment of the available supply of labour and the existing capacity. This creates the possibility of involuntary unemployment in a monetary production economy.

In *The General Theory*, Keynes established the possibility of a monetary production economy stabilizing at a position in which there is involuntary unemployment. It is demand-deficient unemployment. Workers, who are actively seeking employment, are unable to gain employment because there is insufficient aggregate demand to warrant any expansion in the level of output by firms. The behaviour patterns of households and firms are such that, in aggregate, a monetary production economy does not generate automatically a self-adjusting process which results in full employment. This is a unique characteristic of the utilization mode of activity which is dominant within a monetary production economy. It is only within an exchange economy that there is a tendency towards full employment in the absence of structural and informational imperfections. The tendency to move towards a full-employment equilibrium is a unique characteristic of the allocative mode of activity in which the price mechanism ensures generalized market-clearing. In a monetary production economy the multiplier mechanism, not the price mechanism, provides the means of regulation. The inevitable consequence is the possibility of involuntary unemployment. Different contexts of behaviour produce different processes of regulation and hence the possibility of different outcomes.

Prices and wages

The value of any monetary flow equals the associated rate of transactions in quantity terms multiplied by the price per unit transacted. Within a monetary production economy the rate of flow of monetary income regulates itself via the multiplier process. However, the concern of this analysis is to determine the associated levels of output and employment. So far, the conclusions reached on this relationship are only of a provisional nature since any complete analysis requires the explicit introduction of prices and wages. In order to do this, it is necessary to consider the behaviour patterns relating to the determination of price and wage levels within a monetary production economy.

Before addressing the question of how prices and wages are determined, it should be explicitly noted that a dynamic method of analysis is being adopted. Up to this point, a dynamic method has been adopted implicitly. This follows by necessity from the very nature of a monetary production economy. The processes within a monetary production economy are on-going. The concern of any analysis is to deduce the direction of change of these on-going processes as implied by the underlying patterns of behaviour. There is no attempt to explain the actual position at any point in time since it depends on the whole of the previous sequence of dynamic processes. The question 'Why are things currently as they are?' is a matter for historical analysis. The appropriate theoretical question is to discover the processes which are currently operating. 'Why are things currently changing in the ways they are?' Equilibrium analysis can provide a useful theoretical construct with which to investigate the processes of change. Equilibrium analysis is a means of deducing the direction of change implied by the behaviour patterns exhibited within an economy. However, the equilibrium-theoretic approach adopted by classical theory is a static method of analysis. This method is based on the belief that a position at a point in time can be explained solely in terms of the forces operating at that point in time. Such a static method involves the suppression of the time dimension in economic behaviour. It is an analysis which is entirely out of time and, hence, it is entirely inappropriate for understanding the outgoing processes within a monetary production economy. Just as a line is something more than a series of points, so is a dynamic process over time more than a series of static points in time. To reduce behaviour in a monetary production economy to a series of points of static equilibrium, is to deny the significance of the dynamic nature of the context of behaviour.

The difference between the static and the dynamic methods of analysis can be illustrated with reference to the explanation of market price. In classical theory, the demand-and-supply theory of price determination attempts to explain the current level of price in terms of the current state of market demand and supply. In equilibrium, price settles at the level at which the current level of demand equals the current level of supply. The dynamic method of analysis denies the validity of trying to explain the current level of price. Rather, the aim is to explain how the current patterns of behaviour exhibited by firms in their pricing decisions lead to changes in the level of price. The current level of price is itself the outcome of the whole previous sequence of pricing decisions. The static equilibrium-theoretic method of analysis is only a valid theoretical tool in the very special circumstances where the current level of price is set entirely independently of its previous levels. Yet classical theory treats these special circumstances as being true in general. It is yet another example of the failure to recognize the nature of the tacit dimension of knowledge with the inevitable result that a special theory based on a highly restrictive set of presuppositions is viewed, quite mistakenly, as the general theory.

The pricing decision

In the macro exchange economy the aggregate price level is viewed as playing the purely allocative role of ensuring market-clearing on the demand side. In the goods market, the aggregate price level operates through the wealth effect: changes in the aggregate price level imply changes in the real value of the wealth stock of agents, which in turn induce changes in the level of aggregate demand. In the money market the aggregate price level operates in the manner described by the quantity theory of money. In conjunction with the rate of interest, the aggregate price level ensures that the goods and money markets clear simultaneously, thereby generating sufficient aggregate demand with which to maintain the full-employment level of output.

The classical theory of the aggregate price level assumes that firms are the passive transmission mechanisms through which imbalances in demand and supply generate the appropriate allocative price adjustments. Firms are assumed to set prices in such a way as to produce a tendency towards market-clearing on the demand side at the aggregate price level. This heroic assumption implies that firms do not exhibit any non-allocative behaviour patterns. Firms behave as if prices are being set by a Walrasian auctioneer intent on achieving a perfect allocative equilibrium.

The theory of an exchange economy ignores the context of behaviour within which firms actually operate. The theory of a monetary production economy recognizes the significance of the monetary context. Production leads to a monetary outflow in the form of costs. In order to earn profits, firms must pass on these costs plus an added profit margin. Firms need to set their prices such that the monetary inflow of revenue generated per unit of output sold is greater than the monetary outflow of costs incurred. This is mark-up pricing. It is the fundamental behaviour pattern exhibited by firms in the pricing decision in a monetary production economy. Mark-up pricing represents the conductive function of price, the means by which costs are passed on to the purchaser in order to generate profits.

The observation of mark-up pricing, on its own, is insufficient to explain the level of prices. Mark-up pricing leaves the actual price to be set indeterminate since, given the level of costs, price ultimately depends on the size of the profit margin. Firms are likely to have a normal profit margin, the size of which is determined by past custom and practice of individual firms and the individual industries within which they are located. The normal profit margin acts as a benchmark, setting the standard size of the mark-up. The actual size of the mark-up is affected by four other roles which firms may assign to price. The four roles of price, beyond the purely conductive role, are: (1) the allocative role; (2) the positional role; (3) the strategic role; and (4) the financial role.

The allocative role of price is to ensure co-ordination between the level of demand from potential customers and the level of supply of output by firms. This is the role of price on which classical theory has tended to focus. Within the equilibrium-theoretic approach, the demand-and-supply theory of price determination illustrates the allocative role of price in its purest form. If firms are operating in a particular market in which there is excess demand, they can take advantage of these favourable market conditions by seeking to increase their profit margin. This implies higher prices which, in turn, lowers the level of demand. If this process continues, eventually the excess demand is eliminated and market-clearing achieved. Alternatively, if firms face tight market conditions in which there is excess supply, and hence unsold inventories of output, they may react by accepting lower margins and prices. The fall in prices may stimulate the level of demand. Again, if this process continues, eventually the excess supply is eliminated and market-clearing achieved.

If the demand–supply imbalance is generalized across all markets, the aggregate price level tends to rise or fall in an allocative manner. In conditions of generalized excess demand in the aggregate goods markets, firms in all markets tend to raise profit margins and prices. This has the effect of reducing the level of aggregate demand if there is a net negative wealth effect created by the fall in the real value of the wealth stock. On the other hand, in conditions of generalized excess supply in the aggregate goods market, there is a tendency for the aggregate price level to fall as firms across all markets cut margins and prices. This has the effect of increasing aggregate demand if there is a net positive wealth effect created by the rise in the real value of the wealth stock.

The second role of price affecting the size of the mark-up is the positional role in which firms set price to exploit any position of power they have *vis-à-vis* their customers, beyond that created by conditions of excess demand. Such positional power may arise from technological advantages which firms may have over their rivals. Alternatively, positional power may arise from successful competitive strategies which create positions of dominance in which firms are to some extent insulated from the competitive pressures of rival firms. This occurs through effective product differentiation which creates a pool of customers who are 'loyal' to a particular firm's product. This 'loyalty' gives the firm a position of power over its customers which it can exploit. Firms can use any positional power they possess in the form of higher profit margin and, hence, higher prices. Effective product differentiation means that the loss of demand due to higher prices is likely to be relatively low. Furthermore, as costs rise, it is likely that those firms with positional power pass on all the increase in costs in the form of higher prices. The effects of positional power on the level of price are illustrated by classical theory in the static equilibrium-theoretic analysis of monopoly. The theory of monopoly shows that positional power leads to higher prices and lower output than in an allocative equilibrium.

The positional role of price also works in reverse. Firms may be in a position of relative weakness due to technological disadvantages or ineffective product differentiation arising from less successful competitive strategies. Such positions of weakness result in firms facing more intensive competitive pressures from rivals. These firms may have lower profit margins and hence lower prices than otherwise. Furthermore, these firms are less likely to raise prices fully to cover increases in costs.

Classical theory has restricted itself to dealing with only the allocative and positional roles of price. This restricted view of the determination of price is embodied in the structuralist approach to competition. The structuralist hypothesis holds that the behaviour of firms is determined by the structure of the markets within which they operate. Two polar cases of market structure have been developed. The theory of perfect competition provides the pure allocative model of firm behaviour. If a market has a perfectly competitive structure, firms act as allocative co-ordinators ensuring a tendency towards perfect allocative equilibrium. Under conditions of perfect competition the demand-and-supply theory of price determination holds. The other polar case of market structure is that of monopoly. The theory of monopoly provides the pure positional model of price in which there is only one firm within the market. It is the ideal case of perfect dominance.

The theories of perfect competition and monopoly provide the extreme cases at either end of the spectrum of market structure. The structuralist approach to competition holds that it is valid to infer the behaviour of firms in intermediate market structures by determining the position of a particular market structure relative to the two polar cases, with regard to such structural characteristics as concentration, barriers to entry and product differentiation. As market structures become less competitive and more monopolistic, the allocative role of price becomes less significant relative to the positional role. Thus, as the degree of structural imperfection increases, the market outcome moves further and further away from a perfect allocative equilibrium.

The structuralist approach of classical theory abstracts from the complexity of the competitive interactions to be found within the intermediate market structures such as oligopoly. Within an oligopolistic grouping, firms may be engaged in a continuous dynamic process of struggle in which the objective of every firm is to change, in its own favour, the distribution of power within the product group. Within this competitive struggle, price may be used in a variety of tactical ways. This reflects a third role of price, namely the strategic role. It is a role which classical theory does not recognize to have any independent existence. For classical theory, the strategic role of price is but a reflection of the positional power which firms derive from the structural characteristics of their markets. It is the failure of classical theory to recognize the existence of the strategic role of price as a set of influences independent of market structure which accounts for the inability of the classical structuralist approach to generate a more generally applicable theory of oligopoly.

The strategic role of price results from the need of firms to develop competitive strategies with which to achieve their marketing objectives in the face of the competitive strategies adopted by their rivals. Within a competitive strategy, price may be used in many different tactical ways. For example, price may be used within a strategy designed to locate a firm's product within a particular segment in the product group. This tactical use of price can take advantage of the way in which customers treat price as an indicator of quality. A firm wishing to compete from a position within the high-quality segment of the product group, may use a high price as one of the means of positioning itself in that segment.

Another tactical use of price within its strategic function is the setting of price with regard to a portfolio of products. The price for any particular product may be set with regard to a strategy for the whole portfolio of products. For example, a firm may be prepared to accept lower profit margins on a 'leader' product, using that product to build up customer loyalty to the rest of the portfolio. Inasmuch as the 'loss leader' tactic is successful, the prices of the other products in the portfolio can be raised to earn higher-than-normal profit levels.

However, competitive pressures may be such that price is used only very sparingly as a competitive weapon. Price may be a tactic of the last resort. Its very effectiveness in altering the distribution of consumer demand within a product group may render price too dangerous to use, except in the most extreme instances. Firms are normally afraid of provoking an all-out price war, unless they consider themselves strong enough to survive in an even more dominant position. Hence most firms are likely to refrain from lowering price under normal circumstances. This creates a tendency for prices to remain fixed.

A fourth set of influences on the size of the profit margin stem from the use of price to achieve financial objectives. Firms may seek a target rate of return, which implies a particular rate of the firm's monetary profits flow with respect to the monetary value of the firm's asset base. This target rate of return may be determined by the externally imposed constraint that firms need to satisfy the demands of the capital markets in order to maintain the value of their shares.This may require firms to achieve particular rates of dividend payments to shareholders. An alternative financial role of price is to meet internally generated profit objectives. For example, a firm may wish to generate sufficient funds to finance a new investment project or the acquisition of another firm. Inasmuch as a firm wishes to finance investment and acquisitions from internal sources, this may lead the firm to raise its profit margins above the normal levels.

Thus, in summary, the pricing decision in a monetary production economy is a complex matter, involving a number of very different sets of influences. The basic behaviour pattern is that of mark-up pricing, reflecting the conductive role of price in passing on the costs of production. There are, however, a number of other roles for price which can lead to firms altering the size of the mark-up from its normal level. These other roles of price are the allocative, positional, strategic and financial roles. These are a number of interconnections between these non-conductive roles of price. For example, competitive pressures may lead to rigid prices even in conditions of excess demand or rising costs. In these circumstances the strategic role of price completely dominates the allocative and conductive roles, respectively. It is the existence of the qualitatively different behaviour patterns within the pricing decision which renders the structuralist approach invalid as a means of fully understanding the causation of price movements.

The wage bargain

In adopting the theoretical construct of an exchange economy, classical theory fails to recognize the significance of the two features of the context of the wage bargain. First, in a monetary production economy the wage bargain sets the money wage, not the real wage. The real wage is a residual outcome depending on the wage bargain and the aggregate effect of the pricing decision of firms. This is not to say that the participants within the wage bargain do not behave with respect to the real wage. Far from it. Workers are very likely to bargain with reference to the expected real value of any money wage by adopting an expectation about the movement of the aggregate price level. However, the context of the wage bargain is such that it alone does not, and indeed could never, uniquely determine the real wage.

A second feature of the context of the wage bargain in a monetary production economy is that it is a bargain between employers and employees. The wage is not determined as in an auction market with no relationship between buyers and sellers prior to an agreement to trade being reached. The wage bargain takes place within firms between the management and the currently employed workforce. The wage bargain takes place within the context of an on-going relationship between management and workers. It is a bargain which represents the current stage in a historical process. The history of the relationship, by necessity, influences the current wage bargain. History determines the starting-point for the current bargaining process as well as influencing the perceptions and behaviour patterns of the participants. The theoretical economists who ignore these historical factors do so to the peril of their own understanding.

As well as being an historical process, the wage bargain also differs from an auction market by the restriction placed on who can be an active participant. In the wage bargain, participation is limited to those who are currently employed. There is no means by which those who are currently unemployed but actively seeking employment can directly affect the level of money wages. In other words, the context of the wage bargain implies that the money wage is not influenced directly by the allocative pressures which classical theory expects to be generated by an excess supply of labour.

Classical theory has not ignored these features of the context of the wage bargain. It is widely accepted that the peculiar nature of the wage bargain creates the potential for misallocation. Theorists within the classical Keynesian school have developed a number of explanations of misallocation within the labour market. Two broad lines of thought have emerged. One group of theories suggests that the labour market has a dynamically unstable adjustment process which does not tend to result in a market-clearing equilibrium. One reason cited for this dynamic instability is that the relevant price variable for the demand and supply of labour is the real wage, but the price which the wage bargain adjusts, if anything, is the money wage. Another group of theories suggests that misallocation occurs in the labour market because of the peculiar nature of the labour supply function. The exclusive participation of employees within the wage bargain can result in a supply of labour schedule which is perfectly elastic with respect to any downward shift in money wages. This leads to the downward inflexibility of wages even in the face of excess supply in the labour market.

Ultimately, classical theory has sought to explain misallocation in the labour market as the outcome of rational choice under conditions of the structural and/or informational imperfections created by the context of the wage bargain. In so doing classical theory has remained locked into the allocation–misallocation duality. There is no recognition that the context of the wage bargain leads to non-allocative patterns of behaviour which cannot be fully understood from a viewpoint which only allows for allocation and misallocation. The context of the wage bargain creates behaviour patterns which are outside the allocative mode of activity.

The level of money wages at any point in time depends on the whole history of past wage bargains between employers and employees. The current wage bargain is a bargain to change the current money wage. It follows, therefore, that any analysis of the wage bargain must, by necessity, be a dynamic analysis seeking to explain the direction and magnitude of changes in the wage bargain.

In the wage bargain employees have three main bargaining objectives. The first of these objectives is the real-wage objective. Employees seek to maintain the real value of their money wage in the face of any rise in the aggregate price level. This reflects the conductive role of money wages. Employees attempt to pass on any increase in their 'costs' to their employers in order to leave their real position unchanged.

A second objective for employees in the wage bargain is the relative-wage objective. Employees seek to maintain their relative position with regard to other groups of employees. Thus, if one group of employees achieve a particular increase in their money wage, other groups of employees may attempt to match this increase in order to maintain the existing pattern of wage differentials across firms and industries. This concern of employees for their relative position implies that money wages play a strategic role in the sense of being determined, at least partly, by a form of 'competitive' interaction between groups of employees.

A third bargaining objective for employees is the desire to obtain the highest possible absolute increase in the money wage. The maintenance of real and relative wage levels are likely to constitute the minimum outcome of the wage bargain which employees consider as fair and acceptable. Above this minimum acceptable level, employees bargain for the highest possible money wage. Their target level depends on their evaluation of their relative bargaining strength. Employees can derive bargaining strength from the state of labour demand and supply. If employees possess skills which are in short supply, they can attempt to translate this market strength into the achievement of higher money wages. Similarly, if there is generalized excess demand for all types of labour, this can lead to all groups of employees, quite independently, raising their target money wage. The rise in money wages in conditions of excess demand for labour reflects the allocative role of money wages.

Employees may also derive bargaining strength from factors other than excess demand for labour. In such circumstances rises in the money wage play a positional role, reflecting the relative position of power which employees possess *vis-à-vis* their employers. This positional power of employees is likely to come from two main sources. First, employees can derive bargaining strength from any position of strength which firms possess in their product markets. If firms are successful in their product markets, their employees are likely to treat this as an indicator of ability to pay higher wages, and tend, therefore, to adjust their wage demands accordingly. A second important source of bargaining strength for employees is the extent to which firms have invested within their employees through formal training and on-the-job experience. Employees in this position can threaten to leave the firm if the level of money wages paid by the firm is unacceptably low. Faced with the prospect of having to write-off their investment, firms may be prepared to concede the demands for higher wages. The credibility of this threat by skilled employees depends on their ability to obtain alternative employment with acceptable wages and conditions.

Thus employees enter the wage bargain with a number of objectives. They seek a 'fair' outcome, which maintains their real and relative positions as well as reflecting their relative position of strength. The actual bargaining objectives in the current wage bargain are inherently dynamic in nature. The bargaining objectives are prospective in the sense of being based on expectations about the forthcoming period for which the wage agreement will hold. Employees must bargaining on the basis of their expectations about the rate of price inflation and the outcomes of the wage bargains of other groups of employees. The current bargaining objectives are also affected by previous agreements in the sense that employees may include a retrospective element of 'catching up' to compensate for any past failures to achieve their objectives. These past failures may have arisen for two reasons. In the past, firms may have refused to concede fully the wage demands of the employees. Alternatively, the employees may have sought wage demands which in the light of subsequent unexpected events, have turned out to be insufficient. For example, other groups of employees may have achieved unexpectedly high increases in their wage levels or the rate of price inflation may have been higher than previously expected. Thus the current wage demands may contain an element of retrospective correction in the light of the actual historical experience.

These bargaining objectives of workers are likely to result in money wages being inflexible downwards even in conditions of excess supply of labour or a fall in the aggregate price level. This downward inflexibility of wages arises from two factors. First, any wage bargain is particular to one group of employees so that if they accept a wage cut, it implies a reduction in their relative wage. There is no reason for any one group of employees to believe that all other groups will also accept a similar wage cut. Second, the acceptance of a wage cut is in direct conflict with the objective of achieving the highest possible absolute increase in money wages. Wage cuts only arise in extreme circumstances when employees possess no bargaining strength with which to resist their imposition. Under normal circumstances, however, wages tend to exhibit a ratchet effect, with employees always seeking further absolute increases and defending current wage levels against any attempt to reverse the previous gains.

Within the wage bargain, employers seek to limit the rise in money wages to the lowest possible. Employers are normally prepared to concede the minimum acceptable increase to employees required to maintain real and relative wage levels. It is only in extreme cases of competitive weakness when employers may resist even this minimum increase if they believe that the rise in costs will cause a further deterioration in their competitive performance. On the other hand, employers are more likely to concede wage demands in excess of those required for the maintenance of real and relative wage levels if the firm is in a relatively strong competitive position in its product markets, allowing the burden of the wage increases to be passed on to the customer in the form of higher prices. Employers are also more likely to concede wage demands above the minimum acceptable if these wage demands are generalized across all firms in a product group across or the economy as a whole rather than being specific to a particular firm. Employers are also more willing to concede wage demands which are self-financing through employees accepting changes in working practices which lead to improvements in productivity. Such productivity-related wage increases have no effect on the unit costs of production.

Prices, wages and the level of activity

The rate of the money income flow is, by definition, equal to the rate of flow of output multiplied by the aggregate price level. It follows from this definition that the rate of the money income flow changes if there is a change in the rate of the output flow or the aggregate price level or both. There is no implied direction of causality in these statements whatsoever. The direction of causality between the monetary flow, the output flow and the aggregate price level depends on which theory of the economy is adopted.

Classical theory, by assuming that the economy is an exchange economy, imposes a special theory of causation. In equilibrium, the level of output and the aggregate price level are determined simultaneously within the same behavioural process, namely the allocative mode of activity. Output and aggregate price levels adjust to ensure that there is equality between aggregate demand and aggregate supply. The equilibrium outcome of this allocative process is full employment with the aggregate price level adjusting to ensure the sufficiency of aggregate demand, and money wages adjusting, in the light of the aggregate price level, to ensure the market-clearing level of real wages in the labour market. The ultimate determinant of the aggregate price level in an exchange economy is the quantity of money. The rate of the money income flow is seen to be the result of this allocative process.

In a monetary production economy there is no such unique relationship between prices, wages and the level of activity for the reason that there is no single behaviour pattern. In a monetary production economy, prices, wages and the level of activity are also determined quite separately by non-allocative patterns, as well as jointly within any allocative process. The rate of the output flow and the associated level of employment depend on the rate of the monetary flow. Prices and wages play a number of roles beyond the purely allocative, such as the conductive, strategic and positional roles. The rate of the money income flow is therefore the outcome of a whole number of behavioural processes acting quite independently on prices, wages and the level of activity, in addition to the purely allocative interaction of prices and quantities. By remaining wedded to the special case of the allocative interaction of prices and quantities, classical theory has avoided the complexities of the general case.

The two economies compared

The theory of an exchange economy and the theory of a monetary production economy provide two theoretical conceptions of the nature and operation of the capitalist economy. They derive from two alternative frames of reference, embodying entirely different sets of presuppositions on the nature of economic order. The theory of an exchange economy has been developed by the followers of classical theory, the dominant approach in economics. Classical theory views all economic phenomena as being within the allocative mode of activity. The theory of a monetary production economy, on the other hand, offers an alternative perspective, inspired by Keynes's *General Theory*, which recognizes the existence of non-allocative forms of economic behaviour. The theory of a monetary production economy attempts to move beyond the classical allocation–misallocation duality by recognizing the existence of other dimensions of economic order. In particular, prices and quantities are no longer seen to be determined simultaneously in an allocative process with the outcome depending on the structural and informational conditions. The theory of a monetary production economy allows for prices and quantities to be determined quite separately in non-allocative processes.

These differences in the presupposed notions of economic order lead to very different views on the operation of the macro economy. In a macro exchange economy, the equilibrium outcome is determined, ultimately, by the supply side. In particular, the allocative mechanism in the labour market ensures a tendency towards a full-employment equilibrium, while the allocative mechanisms on the demand side ensure that there is sufficient aggregate demand to maintain the full-employment level of aggregate supply. However, in a monetary production economy, the macro equilibrium is determined by the demand side. The multiplier process determines the rate of flow of aggregate demand, which in turn determines the rate of the productive flow and, hence, the current level of employment. There is no reason whatsoever why the demand side in a monetary production economy should tend to generate a rate of monetary flow consistent with the full-employment rate of the productive flow. Thus, at the macro level, an exchange economy and a monetary production economy exhibit reverse causal sequences. In the exchange economy, the supply side determines the demand side, this causal sequence being summed up by Say's Law, that supply creates its own demand. In a monetary production economy, the causal sequence is reversed with the demand side determining the supply side: demand creates its own supply.

Another fundamental difference between the two economies lies in the respective presuppositions about the nature of money. In an exchange economy the quantity of money is exogenously determined. It is a parameter of the system under the control of the central monetary authorities. As the supply of money changes, this initiates an allocative process within the exchange economy with equilibrium being restored through adjustments in the aggregate price level (as captured in the quantity theory of money) and the rate of interest (as captured in the theory of liquidity preference). It follows, therefore, that in an exchange economy the quantity of money ultimately determines the rate of flow of money income. The quantity of money is the crucial exogenous variable determining, in turn, the aggregate price level and the rate of the monetary flow.

In a monetary production economy, however, the direction of causality is entirely reversed. The rate of the monetary flow depends on the separate behavioural processes which determine the aggregate price level and the rate of the output flow. It is the rate of the monetary flow which determines the quantity of money required. Unless the central monetary authorities impose restrictions, money is always automatically created within a monetary production economy on demand by households and firms. Money is the medium for exchange. The quantity of money is entirely demand-determined, not demand-determining. Monetary production economies possess the potential to create the necessary monetary means for conducting transactions. The actual amount created depends on the rate of monetary flow. It is this separation between the potential and the actual which makes the quantity of money such a theoretical, and empirical, will-o'-the-wisp. From a non-classical perspective, the notion of some exogenously determined supply of money is a myth arising from the classical presumption that a capitalist economy behaves as if it is an exchange economy.

The difference in the nature of money in the two economies is most apparent over the issue of neutrality. In an exchange economy, the equilibrium outcome is full employment, irrespective of the prevailing monetary conditions. Money is neutral with respect to the equilibrium level of real variables. This neutrality is the logical implication of the classical presupposition that money is a non-essential aspect of the context of economic behaviour. The theory of a monetary production economy starts from the entirely opposite presupposition that money is an essential aspect of the context of economic behaviour, giving rise to the behaviour patterns exhibited. Far from being neutral with respect to real variables, it is the monetary context which creates the behaviour patterns that, in turn, determine output and employment levels. Classical theory deduces the neutrality of money within a theoretical analysis of economic behaviour in a non-monetary context. It is hardly surprising that an analysis which presupposes that money is peripheral should ultimately arrive at the theoretical conclusion that money is indeed peripheral. What is remarkable is the failure on the part of the followers of classical theory to admit that the 'discovery' of the neutrality property is little more than the uncovering of their own, still unacknowledged, presuppositions. Logical analysis is, after all is said and done, only a set of rules for deducing the implications of what has been assumed in the first place. Change the premises and the implications are likely to change. The neutrality property of money is entirely the result of a particular restrictive presupposition adopted by classical theory.

4

The Capitalist Economy

The structure of the capitalist economy

The capitalist economy is characterized by the existence of a stock of capital which has been accumulated over time. This accumulated stock of capital is used to generate a monetary return in the current period. The capital stock consists of two different types of capital: productive capital and non-productive capital. The stock of productive capital is made up of industrial plant and machinery used to produce goods and services. Productive capital provides a monetary return in the form of profits by being used to generate a revenue inflow from the sale of output in excess of the outflow arising from the incurred costs of production.

The stock of non-productive capital consists of two different forms of capital: financial assets and real assets. Financial assets are either monetary or non-monetary in form. Monetary financial assets (such as notes and coins) and demand bank deposits represent an accumulated stock of purchasing power. Non-monetary financial assets (such as time bank deposits, shares and government securities) represent purchasing power which has been temporarily transferred to other agents in the economy. In return for giving up, temporarily, the use of their purchasing power to borrowers, holders of non-monetary financial assets receive a rate of interest. They may also be able to make capital gains (or losses) if a market exists for buying and selling the particular type of non-monetary financial asset which they hold. If the market value of a particular type of non-monetary financial asset increases, capital gains accrue to the owners of that type of asset. The second form of non-productive capital are real assets, such as land, houses and precious metals, which are not used for productive purposes. Markets exist for buying and selling these real assets so that they can generate a return in the form of capital gains if their market value increases.

The existence of two types of capital, productive and non-productive, is reflected in the structure of the capitalist economy. The capitalist economy can be considered to be made up of two fundamental sectors: the industrial sector and the financial sector. The industrial sector is defined in a wide sense to include all those activities concerned with the generation of profits by firms using their stock of productive capital. Thus the industrial sector is used in the present analysis to cover all productive activities in the primary, secondary and tertiary sectors of the capitalist economy. Within the industrial sector activities can be separated into those concerned with the demand side and those concerned with the supply side. Demand-side activities involve the decisions by households to purchase consumer goods and services and the decisions by firms to purchase investment goods, that is currently-produced productive capital. On the supply side, firms must decide on the rate of the output flow of goods and services and the associated level of employment of the labour supply of households. The activities of the industrial sector result in the circular flow of money income.

The financial sector, on the other hand, consists of all those activities generated by the use of the non-productive capital stock to create a monetary return. This involves all owners of non-productive capital in the portfolio decision of how to hold their wealth. They must choose between the various forms of non-productive asset, both financial and real. This portfolio decision results in the buying and selling of different assets on their respective markets.

The two sectors are not independent. They interact, primarily through the savings–investment relationship. Savings represent that part of the monetary flow in the industrial sector which leaks out of the sector into the financial sector. The decision to save is the decision to accumulate more non-productive capital at the expense of purchasing currently produced goods and services. Externally financed investment, on the other hand, represents an injection into the monetary flow in the industrial sector from the financial sector. The decision to invest is the decision to utilize purchasing power stored as non-productive capital in order to accumulate currently-produced productive capital. The capitalist economy can be considered to be in dynamic balance if there is no net flow of funds to and from the industrial and financial sectors.

The classical view of the capitalist economy

The classical frame of reference views the capitalist economy as an exchange economy, made up of a series of interdependent markets. All economic behaviour is considered as a process of stock adjustment regulated by the price mechanism. In the absence of any structural or informational imperfections, price tends to the market-clearing level in the manner described by the demand-and-supply theory of price determination. It follows that prices and quantities are seen as being determined simultaneously within this process of stock adjustment.

Classical theory has developed within one particular frame of reference, making the tacit assumption that this frame of reference is the necessary and sufficient theoretical means for understanding the capitalist economy. Thus the classical view has emerged that the theory of the exchange economy is the only valid and complete theory of the capitalist economy. In holding to this belief, classical theory has adopted a unitary view of the capitalist economy. No fundamental difference is seen between economic behaviour in the industrial sector and economic behaviour in the financial sector. The context of behaviour is the same within both sectors, namely that agents are involved in a process of stock adjustment. Thus the behaviour of agents in both sectors is considered to be within the allocative mode of activity.

In the industrial sector, classical theory views the supply side as being regulated by the labour market. By means of real-wage adjustment, the demand for labour by firms is brought into equality with the supply of labour by households. Thus the labour market generates a tendency towards a full-employment level of output on the supply side of the industrial sector.

For the industrial sector to be in equilibrium overall there must be sufficient aggregate demand to purchase the full-employment level of output. In the early stages of its theoretical development, classical theory proposed the loanable funds market as the means by which the demand side in the industrial sector is regulated. Sufficient aggregate demand in the goods market is achieved via interest rate adjustment in the loanable funds market. The rate of interest acts as a price mechanism ensuring that the flow of funds from the industrial sector to the financial sector in the form of savings by households, is exactly balanced by a flow of funds in the opposite direction in the form of borrowings to finance investment expenditure by firms.

The classical theory of the demand side in the industrial sector was extended in the light of Keynesian criticisms of the effectiveness of the rate of interest in ensuring a sufficient level of investment to sustain the level of aggregate demand required for full employment. These Keynesian criticisms led to the proposition that there is a dual adjustment mechanism on the demand side in the industrial sector. In addition to the rate of interest, the aggregate price level would also regulate the level of aggregate demand in the goods market through the wealth effect.

When it comes to the analysis of the operation of the financial sector, classical theory did not initially see this sector as a significant influence on the behaviour of the macro exchange economy. Classical theory only considered the financial sector with regard to the flow of funds between the industrial and financial sectors in form of savings and investment, these flows being regulated in the loanable funds market by interest rate adjustment. Beyond this savings–investment relationship, the operation of the financial sector was largely ignored by early classical theories. Indeed, classical theory adopted the view that the crucial separation in the capitalist economy is between the real sector and the monetary sector. The industrial sector and its savings–investment relationship with the financial sector fall within the real sector. The monetary sector consists of a money market in which the aggregate price level acts as the means by which the transactions demand for money is brought into equality with the exogenously determined supply of money. It is this allocative process in the money market which is captured in the quantity theory of money.

Classical theory developed a fuller treatment of the macro implications of the financial sector following the emergence of the Keynesian school of thought. Keynesian theory recognized that the operation of the financial sector involved the allocation of a stock of wealth between a number of competing forms in which this stock of wealth could be stored. Keynesian theory represents this portfolio decision as a choice between money and bonds, thus recognizing the role of money as a store of value. In the Keynesian theory of liquidity preference, the rate of interest is seen as the means by which market-clearing is achieved in the money and bonds markets simultaneously. Thus in the extended form of the classical theory the aggregate price level and the rate of interest act as a dual adjustment mechanism ensuring generalized market-clearing in the financial sector.

Thus, classical theory, in its modern form, provides an analysis of the macro exchange economy in which the real wage, the aggregate price level and the rate of interest are the allocative mechanisms ensuring a tendency for the economy to move to a position of generalized equilibrium with, by implication, a full-employment level of activity. From this perspective, Keynes's *General Theory* is viewed as remaining within the classical frame of reference within which Keynes is seen to have provided an analysis of how the portfolio allocation process in the financial sector is regulated by the rate of interest. This, in turn, led Keynes to develop a more sophisticated analysis of the process of macro misallocation, resulting ultimately from the existence of structural and informational imperfections at the micro level. Those classical Keynesians, who view Keynes in classical terms, reject, at least implicitly, the notion that Keynes's *General Theory* marked any departure from the unitary view of the capitalist economy held by classical theorists.

The significance of Keynes's *General Theory*

Most interpretations of Keynes's *General Theory* have been from within the classical frame of reference. Keynes's *General Theory* has inspired the search for the classical microfoundations which lead to the appearance of involuntary unemployment. Under what conditions does the behaviour of rational economic agents result in an underemployment equilibrium? The search for this Keynesian holy grail has been undertaken by the classical Keynesian school of thought, which has sought to develop an orthodox synthesis in which Keynes's insights are incorporated within the classical set of presupposed notions of economic order. Thus Keynes's *General Theory* has come to be seen as a theory of macro misallocation in the exchange economy. The classical Keynesian school of thought has elaborated the imperfectionist theories of misallocation in an exchange economy, showing how structural and informational imperfections at the micro level can lead to misallocation at the macro level. The result of this research programme has been the emasculation of the characteristic Keynesian proposition that involuntary unemployment is caused by a lack of aggregate demand. This proposition was reduced to an extreme case of peripheral theoretical importance within the so-called Neoclassical Synthesis. In this view, deficient aggregate demand arose only if there is interest rate maladjustment on the demand side. Even this very limited proposition was subsequently undermined by the notion that the aggregate price level would, via the wealth effect, ensure sufficient aggregate demand to support the full-employment level of output. It followed from the Neoclassical Synthesis that, in general, involuntary unemployment is caused by real wage maladjustment in the labour market resulting from the downward rigidity of the money wage, one possible cause of this supply-side maladjustment being the structural imperfection created by the existence of monopoly power in the form of trade unions. More recently, classical Keynesian theories have dealt with the maladjustment of the price mechanism arising from informational imperfections. Thus, for the classical Keynesians, Keynes's *General Theory* has acted as but a grain of sand in the classical oyster, provoking developments within classical theory which have increased the beauty and sophistication of classical theory, the imperfectionist theories of misallocation being the resulting classical pearls of wisdom.

An alternative starting-point for understanding Keynes's *General Theory* is to interpret Keynes as having made a revolutionary break from classical theory. Keynes's *General Theory* can be interpreted as the rejection of the classical frame of reference as the appropriate theoretical means with which to understand the causes of mass unemployment in the capitalist economy. Keynes can be seen as reaching this rejection of the classical theory of unemployment on behavioural grounds. Keynes's *General Theory*, in this view, is a theory based on the belief that firms and households exhibit patterns of behaviour which are qualitatively different from the allocative mode of activity. Thus Keynes can be seen as rejecting the choice-theoretic method of analysis, in which all economic behaviour is treated as optimizing choices made by rational economic agents. The building blocks of Keynes's *General Theory* are empirically based generalizations about the patterns of behaviour which are actually followed by firms and households. Keynes's *General Theory* is not based upon the orthodox microfoundations of theoretical fictions in the form of rational agents making optimizing choices.

The adoption of the behavioural approach by Keynes led to the rejection of the classical theory of the exchange economy as the appropriate theory for understanding the operation of the industrial sector. This resulted in Keynes developing the theory of a monetary production economy in which recognition is given to the significance of the monetary context of behaviour within the industrial sector of a capitalist economy. The theory of monetary production economy deduces the implications of the behaviour patterns of firms and households operating with respect to monetary flows. It is this theory which Keynes began to elaborate in the *General Theory*. In so doing Keynes made the crucial theoretical discovery that the multiplier process is the means of regulation within a monetary production economy.

Keynes's analysis of the behaviour of firms and households within the industrial sector implied the rejection of the price mechanism as the means of regulation. In particular, Keynes denied the existence of a labour market in the classical sense of employment and wage levels being determined simultaneously within an allocative process. Keynes realized that employment and wage levels are determined in separate processes of behaviour. The level of employment depends, ultimately, on the level of aggregate demand. A monetary production economy is a demand-side economy in which demand determines supply, unlike an exchange economy, in which the supply side is the driving force. The real wage does not play an allocative role ensuring that the demand for labour equals the supply of labour. The demand for labour depends on the level of aggregate demand, not the level of the real wage. Furthermore, as Keynes recognized, the real wage is but a residual outcome, depending on the wage bargain and the pricing decision. The wage bargain determines the money wage, not the real wage. There is no reason why the money wage should move in response to an allocative imbalance between labour demand and supply. Indeed, Keynes postulated that the maintenance of relative wage levels is the primary force operating in the wage bargain. The belief that employment and wage levels are determined separately in non-allocative patterns of behaviour, is tantamount to denying the existence of an aggregate market for labour.

Keynes's analysis of the industrial sector also implies the denial of the existence of a loanable funds market. The rate of interest is not the price mechanism which ensures the level of investment equals the level of savings, so that there is no net flow of funds between the industrial and financial sectors. In a monetary production economy, the investment–savings interaction is not an allocative process regulated by the price mechanism. Rather, it is changes in the rate of the monetary flow itself which is the means of regulating the flow of funds between the industrial and financial sectors.

The denial of the existence of the labour market and the loanable funds market by Keynes represents the rejection of the classical theory of the industrial sector. The classical approach is not applicable to understanding the behaviour patterns within the industrial sector which determine the level of activity in a capitalist economy. In particular, the industrial sector is not characterized by a market-theoretic context of behaviour. Quite simply, Keynes's *General Theory* can be interpreted as the denial that classical theory can offer an explanation of the causes of mass unemployment in a capitalist economy.

This interpretation of Keynes's *General Theory* does not imply that Keynes believed that classical theory had no validity whatsoever. Keynes rejected classical theory in a limited sense. Keynes rejected classical theory with regard to its analysis of the determination of the aggregate level of activity in the industrial sector on the grounds that the aggregate level of activity is not determined in an allocative process in the labour market and the loanable funds market. This criticism of classical theory does not imply that there are no allocative processes at all in the capitalist economy. Indeed, Keynes believed quite the reverse. For example, classical theory could provide an analysis of the micro processes involved in the determination of the distribution of resources between different types of industrial activities under conditions of a full-employment level of aggregate activity.

Furthermore, Keynes retained the classical approach for his analysis of the operation of the financial sector. The context of behaviour in the financial sector is that of an exchange economy. In the financial sector agents are faced with a portfolio decision. They must choose in which form to hold their accumulated stock of financial wealth given the alternative forms of assets available. Thus agents are involved in a process of stock adjustment. This is the allocative mode of activity for which classical theory is the appropriate means of analysis. Using the classical approach, Keynes developed the theory of liquidity preference, in which the rate of interest is the price mechanism which ensures market-clearing simultaneously in the money and bond markets. The theory of liquidity preference is a classical theory of allocation.

If this non-classical interpretation of Keynes's *General Theory* is accepted, the revolutionary achievement of Keynes is his move away from the unitary view of the capitalist economy held by classical theory. In *The General Theory*, very different theories are proposed to explain the operation of the industrial and financial sectors. Keynes explains the operation of the industrial sector by the theory of a monetary production economy in which the multiplier process acts as the means of regulation. On the other hand, Keynes retains classical theory as the starting-point for explaining the operation of the financial sector. The financial sector is an exchange economy in which the allocative process of stock adjustment is regulated by a price mechanism. Thus, from this non-classical perspective, Keynes's *General Theory* points the way forward to a theory of the capitalist economy in which the limitations to the classical frame of reference are clearly recognized. This is the real significance of *The General Theory*.

A theory of the capitalist economy

Classical theory treats the capitalist economy as an exchange economy characterized by only one mode of activity, namely the allocative mode of activity. In adopting the theory of an exchange economy as the theory of a capitalist economy, classical theory does not recognize any fundamental difference between the contexts of behaviour within which industrial and financial capital must operate. Thus classical theory can be said to adopt a unitary view of the capitalist economy.

The present analysis represents a break from this unitary view of the capitalist economy provided by classical theory. The fundamental proposition is that the monetary context of behaviour in the industrial sector leads to non-allocative forms of economic behaviour which are qualitatively different from the allocative mode of activity of an exchange economy. Once it is accepted that there are non-allocative forms of economic behaviour, the theory of an exchange economy is no longer an adequate theoretical representation of the capitalist economy. The theory of a monetary production economy becomes the appropriate starting-point for the study of behaviour in the industrial sector.

The most significant consequence of the monetary context of behaviour in the industrial sector is that it creates a utilization problem for industrial capital. This utilization problem is a unique characteristic of industrial capital. Unlike financial capital, industrial capital can be underutilized. It is possible for a part of the stock of industrial capital to be inactive in the sense of not being used to generate a rate of return. Thus the managers of the stock of industrial capital face a decision on the level of utilization in addition to the more allocative-type problem over the specific forms in which to hold the stock of industrial capital.

This inactive part of the stock of industrial capital does not refer to that part which exists for usage only in temporary periods of above normal utilization. This type of idle industrial capital is entirely intentional, arising from precautionary motives on the part of firms. The problem of underutilization refers to unintentional non-usage of industrial capital, which firms seek to avoid. Henceforth, full utilization of industrial capital is defined to include any non-usage of that capacity which exists for precautionary reasons.

There are two possible types of constraint on the level of utilization of industrial capital. These constraints may lead to a part of the stock of industrial capital being inactive and therefore unable to generate a flow of profits. The first type of constraint is a supply-side one, arising from a shortage of labour. It is possible that the accumulation of industrial capital may eventually outstrip the growth in the supply of labour to such an extent that there is insufficient labour with which to fully utilize the stock of industrial capital. In the short-run, this labour shortage constraint may be partially overcome by a rise in the level of real wages, which may lead to an increase in the supply of labour. In the longer-run, persistent labour shortage may be resolved by an increase in the supply of labour arising either from higher participation rates or the inward migration of population. Alternatively, labour shortages may be resolved through technical progress in the methods of production. Such process innovation may lead to lower labour requirements per unit of industrial capital. The problem of supply-side constraints on the level of utilization are beyond the short-run concerns of the present analysis. Thus, following Keynes, it is assumed that the size of the existing stock of industrial capital is just sufficient to ensure the full employment of all those available and actively seeking employment. Under this simplifying assumption, the full utilization of the stock of industrial capital implies the full employment of the available supply of labour, and vice versa.

A second cause of underutilization of industrial capital is the demand-side constraint imposed if there is insufficient aggregate demand. This demand-side constraint arises from the monetary context of behaviour within which the managers of industrial capital operate. The implications of the context of behaviour are explained by Keynes in his theory of a monetary production economy contained in *The General Theory*. The level of utilization of industrial capital depends on the level of demand which firms expect to exist for their products. As Keynes showed, the level of aggregate demand in a monetary production economy is regulated by the multiplier process. A monetary production economy tends to move towards a position of dynamic balance in which there is sufficient aggregate demand to purchase the aggregate supply of output. This is achieved by changes in the rate of the monetary flow. As this rate of flow adjusts, the level of activity may change and hence lead to a change in the rate of utilization of the stock of industrial capital. This creates the possibility that a monetary production economy may tend towards a position of dynamic balance in which the level of aggregate demand is such as to imply the involuntary unemployment of labour and the involuntary underutilization of industrial capital.

The utilization mode of activity is a unique characteristic of the industrial sector. The theory of a monetary production economy provides an explanation of this mode of activity which is beyond the scope of classical theory. In analysing the industrial sector, classical theory reduces the utilization mode of activity to the purely allocative mode of activity. Thus classical theory believes that the allocative process of real-wage adjustment in the labour market ensures that the aggregate supply of output is at the full utilization level or moving automatically towards it. Furthermore, the allocative process of adjustment of the rate of interest and the aggregate price level in the goods market ensures that there is sufficient aggregate demand to purchase the full-utilization level of output. In providing such an analysis of the industrial sector, classical theory fails to recognize that underutilization is not caused by imperfection blocking the price mechanisms which regulate the allocative processes. The industrial sector just does not operate in that way. These price mechanisms do not exist. Classical theory cannot see that the context of behaviour within the industrial sector gives rise to non-allocative modes of activity. Classical theory looks at the world through the classical frame of reference and sees, not surprisingly, a world of allocation and misallocation. Its frame of reference does not allow it to see anything else. To see the utilization mode of activity requires another frame of reference, a frame of reference which Keynes began to provide in his theory of a monetary production economy.

The theory of a monetary production economy provides the starting-point for the theory of behaviour in the industrial sector, particularly the utilization problem facing industrial capital. But it does not follow from this that the theory of a monetary production economy provides an adequate theory of the capitalist economy. To make such a claim is to remain wedded to the sort of methodological stance which underlies classical theory, maintaining a bounded vision with regard to the limitations inherent in any one set of presupposed notions of order, albeit a bounded vision from a non-classical perspective. A second fundamental proposition of the present analysis is that the theory of a monetary production economy is inadequate with regard to providing an understanding of the operation of the financial sector. In the financial sector the management of financial capital involves the decision on how to distribute a stock of financial capital between the alternative forms in which wealth may be stored. This portfolio decision leads to an allocative process of stock adjustment. The context of behaviour in the financial sector is such that financial capital does not face a utilization problem. The stock of financial capital is always fully utilized in the sense of fulfilling the function of providing a means of storing purchasing power. The whole of the stock of financial capital is always generating a rate of return by the very virtue of being a stock. Thus no part of the stock of financial capital is ever idle or inactive, unlike industrial capital. The rate of return from financial capital can be said to depend only on the form in which it is utilized, not the extent of its utilization.

From this preliminary treatment of the financial sector as being characterized by an allocative process of stock adjustment, it follows that the classical theory of an exchange economy provides the appropriate starting-point for the analysis of behaviour in the financial sector. The following chapter gives a far more detailed treatment of the financial sector in which the financial sector is seen as involving elements of an exchange economy in conjunction with elements of a monetary production economy. None the less, the overall conclusion is unaffected. The capitalist economy should not be treated in a unitary manner as in classical theory. It is more appropriate to adopt a dualistic view of the capitalist economy which recognizes the existence of two very different contexts of behaviour in the capitalist economy. The monetary context of behaviour in the industrial sector (and part of the financial sector) requires the use of the theory of a monetary production economy, whereas the market-theoretic context of behaviour in the financial sector requires the use of the classical theory of an exchange economy.

The crucial first step towards this dualist view of the capitalist economy is provided by Keynes's *General Theory*. Keynes rejected the classical notion that the industrial sector is regulated in an allocative manner by the price mechanism. Keynes denied the existence at the macro level of a market for labour and a market for loanable funds in the classical allocative sense. In place of the classical approach, Keynes developed the theory of a monetary production economy as the appropriate frame of reference for understanding the industrial sector. This shows that the levels of output and employment depend on the level of aggregate demand as regulated by the multiplier process. This implies a reversal of the traditional view of causation. In the exchange economy it is the supply side in the form of the labour market which ultimately determines the point of equilibrium. This is encapsulated in Say's Law that supply creates its own demand. In the monetary production economy, on the other hand, demand creates its own supply. Keynes, however, retained the classical approach for explaining the operation of the financial sector. The Keynesian theory of liquidity preference views the rate of interest as an allocative mechanism ensuring that the demand for money equals the supply of money. Thus Keynes adopted a dualistic approach to the theory of the capitalist economy in which the industrial sector is treated as a monetary production economy but the financial sector is treated as an exchange economy. This is the Keynesian dual-economy thesis, the principal building-block of the present analysis.

The present analysis has attempted to extend the initial analysis presented by Keynes in *The General Theory* in at least four ways. First, the present analysis is explicitly based on the need to adopt behavioural and dynamic methods of analysis. Second, the theory of a monetary production economy has been much extended, particularly in respect of incorporating fully the non-allocative roles of prices and wages. Much of this analysis on the conductive, strategic and positional roles of prices and wages was never addressed in Keynes's initial analysis of a monetary production economy. Third, the present analysis will, in the subsequent chapter, highlight the dual nature of the financial sector arising from the differences in the operation of the banking system and the stock market system. Finally, the supply of money is treated as an endogenous, demand-determined variable. Although a common theme in post-Keynesian monetary theory, Keynes himself, in the presentation of the theory of liquidity preference, adopted the traditional classical assumption of an exogenously determined money supply.

The dualistic nature of the capitalist economy implies the need to move beyond the macro theories of classical theory. Classical theory provides a theory of an exchange economy. It is therefore only applicable to the operation of the financial sector, the only arena of the allocative mode of activity in the macro capitalist economy. In order to provide a macro theory of the industrial sector, it is necessary to develop alternative, non-classical, theories which allow for non-allocative behaviour patterns. The theory of a monetary production economy provides just such a theory in which prices and wages play non-allocative roles and economic behaviour is regulated by non-allocative mechanisms.

Thus the dualistic nature of the capitalist economy requires a revolutionary synthesis in which the limits to the relevance of the classical frame of reference are clearly defined, and alternative but complementary frames of reference are introduced to explain non-allocative forms of behaviour. Such a revolutionary synthesis marks the beginning of a post-classical economics in which the bounded vision of the classical frame of reference is overcome. Keynes's *General Theory* marked the first vital step towards this post-classical synthesis, but sadly, the majority of economists have never made the journey, content instead to remain within the comfortable surroundings of their orthodox system of beliefs. Thus they have succeeded only in further developing the theory of an exchange economy. Until they are prepared to move beyond their own self-imposed but unacknowledged limits, economic theory will never produce a really adequate theory of the capitalist economy, developing the theoretical revolution initiated by Keynes's *General Theory*.

5

The Financial Sector

The nature of the financial sector

The context of behaviour in the financial sector is one in which a stock of wealth has to be allocated between different types of assets. Agents in the financial sector face a portfolio decision. They must decide how to hold their stock of wealth, given the range of assets available. The continual revision of these portfolio decisions generates a stock-adjustment process as agents substitute different types of assets within their portfolio of asset holdings.

Within this stock-adjustment process in the financial sector, financial institutions act as intermediaries, undertaking many of the portfolio allocation decisions of individual agents. Financial institutions are able to acquire control of the stocks of wealth of individual agents by offering the advantages of scale and scope in the form of lower per unit transactions costs and risk-spreading. Financial institutions use their financial capital to generate profits from the portfolio allocation process by obtaining a monetary return in excess of that which they pay to individual investors.

The stock of wealth to be allocated at any point in time consists of the stock of wealth accumulated prior to the current period plus the net addition to the stock of wealth from the current monetary flow. This increment to the stock of wealth has two components. First, the stock of wealth is increased by savings, that part of current money income which agents have decided not to use for expenditure purposes during the current period. The stock of wealth is also increased temporarily by that part of current money income as yet unspent but which agents plan to use for expenditure purposes during the current period. These temporary transactions balances arise from the non-coincidence in time of current income inflows and current expenditure out-flows.

In making their portfolio decisions, agents face a choice between a whole range of different types of assets. Within this range of assets are real and financial assets. Agents may choose to hold their wealth in the form of real assets such as property, precious metals and antiques. Such assets can provide a flow of real services in addition to their 'store-of-value' function. Financial assets, on the other hand, are 'paper' claims to wealth created in the process of storing accumulated purchasing power. Some types of financial assets such as notes and coins act only as stores of purchasing power. Other types of financial assets, such as bank deposits and government securities, act as stores of purchasing power but also involve the temporary transfer of purchasing power to other agents. Agents may temporarily transfer their accumulated purchasing power to other agents by one of two methods. The first method of transfer is debt. The recipients of the transfer of purchasing power undertake to repay the amount borrowed at some future date. Thus wealth holders receive a 'paper' claim to repayment. The period of repayment varies between different types of debt. In the case of some types of bank deposits, repayment is immediate on demand, while at the other extreme there are perpetuities with an infinitely long repayment period.

Another method of transfer of purchasing power is the equity one. A company can raise finance by a new equity issue in which wealth holders provide funds in exchange for a share in the ownership of the assets of the company. If the assets of the company are real, as in the case of the plant and machinery of industrial firms, the purchase of equity represents the arm's-length purchase of real assets.

Financial assets can be categorized as monetary or non-monetary. Monetary financial assets are those financial stores of purchasing power which can be used immediately as a medium of exchange. Notes and coins are examples of monetary financial assets as are types of bank deposits on which cheques may be written. Non-monetary financial assets are financial stores of purchasing power which cannot be used immediately as a medium of exchange. Non-monetary financial assets need to be exchanged into a monetary form before their purchasing power can actually be realized.

Real and financial assets can generate two types of monetary return: (1) service payments and (2) changes in capital values. Service payments represent the payments which wealth holders receive every period for the use of their wealth. In the case of financial assets, wealth holders receive interest payments on debt, and dividend payments on equity. Service payments on real assets can only be earned in the form of rent payments from the temporary transfer to other agents of the usage rights of these assets.

An alternative source of monetary return from real and financial assets results from changes in their capital values. If a market exists to trade a particular type of asset, this creates the possibility of capital gains or losses for agents as the market value of the particular asset varies.

Although the context of behaviour in the financial sector is the allocation of the stock of wealth between different types of assets, it does not follow that there is a unitary mode of activity throughout the financial sector. Indeed, it is a crucial characteristic if the financial sector that it is itself dualistic in nature, being made up of two systems which operate in different ways. These two systems are the banking system and the stock-market system. The existence of these two systems within the financial sector means that it is invalid to characterize that sector of the capitalist economy as being wholly within the allocative mode of activity. The financial sector is not a pure exchange economy in which the stock-adjustment process is regulated within markets by the price mechanism. The adoption of this dualistic view of the financial sector represents a move beyond Keynes's analysis of the financial sector, but a move which could be considered to be within the spirit of Keynes.

The banking system

The banking system acts as an intermediary in the debt method of transferring purchasing power. Banks and other similar institutions offer bank deposits as one form of financial asset. Banks relend these deposits to other agents in the form of bank loans and credit facilities. Profits are generated from the differential between the rate of interest received on loans and the rate of interest paid out on deposits.

Bank deposits are a non-traded form of financial asset. Hence their capital value is fixed so that there is no scope for any capital gains or losses. The only monetary return on bank deposits are the interest payments which may be received on them. However, bank deposits offer a non-monetary return in the form of liquidity. Bank deposits are highly liquid in the sense of being readily convertible into a means of exchange with virtually no risk of non-repayment in full. Bank deposits can be fully repaid to the wealth holder on immediate demand at zero cost or, at most, with reduced interest payments. Indeed, some types of bank deposits can be used directly as a means of exchange.

There are five main sources of funds available to the banking system in the current period:

1 The stock of bank deposits accumulated prior to the current period.
2 The net inflow of funds from the industrial sector.
3 The net inflow of funds from the rest of the financial sector.
4 The interest payments on bank deposits which agents retain as deposits.
5 The retained earnings of the banks themselves.

The amount of funds from each of these sources is likely to be determined by a wide range of factors. For example, the previously accumulated stock of bank deposits is the result of the whole historical process prior to the current period. The net inflow of funds from the industrial sector consists of two components: temporary transactions balances and net savings. Following the Keynesian behavioural assumptions, it is likely that the rates of both of these inflows vary directly with the current rate of the monetary flow. The main determinant of the net flow of funds to or from the rest of the financial sector is likely to be the relative rates of return offered by the banking system and other forms of assets.

The rate of inflow of new funds to the banking system is also likely to be affected by the level of uncertainty which agents have with regards to the future. Agents save partly as a hedge against 'a rainy day'. This is what Keynes referred to as the precautionary motive in the demand for money. As uncertainty increases about the future, a larger proportion of the current monetary flow may come to the banking system. The aggregate outcome of such a behaviour pattern will be a reduction of aggregate demand and, as a consequence, a fall in output and employment. It is an example of a self-fulfilling prophecy, a characteristic of much economic behaviour under conditions of uncertainty. The rate of inflow of funds to the banking system may also vary with the rate of price inflation, inasmuch as agents seek to maintain some notional real stock of bank deposits. Such a behaviour pattern may be related to concerns about the future. Higher price inflation may be treated as an indicator that the future is more uncertain.

The current stock of bank deposits provides the banking system with its supply of loanable funds, subject to the restriction imposed by the need to retain a portion of the total value of deposits in the form of liquid assets rather than loans in order to cover for the withdrawal of deposits. The size of this liquidity ratio is determined either by the banks themselves on the basis of experience or by the regulations of the central monetary authorities.

The demand for loanable funds in the current period is made up of two elements:

1 The existing stock of outstanding loans made prior to the current period.
2 The demand for new loans during the current period.

The demand for new loans is in turn made up of two different types of demand. First there is the demand for temporary transactions loans. These loans are used to bridge the gap in time between expenditure outflows and income inflows. These loans are repaid within the current period. They are the debt alternative to temporary transactions balances, which play the same role but in circumstances in which income leads expenditure. The second type of demand for new loans comes from agents who seek to finance expenditure with bank loans which are to be repaid over future periods. This loan-financed expenditure may be used to purchase either currently produced goods and services or existing real and financial assets.

Just as with the supply of funds to the banking system, the determination of the level of demand for loanable funds involves a whole range of factors. The existing stock of accumulated loans is the outcome of the historical process prior to the current period. Following the Keynesian behavioural assumptions, both the level of temporary transactions loans and the demand for loans of finance expenditure on currently produced goods and services are likely to be primarily determined by the current rate of the monetary flow. The demand for loans to finance the purchase of existing assets is likely to depend on the rates of return from these assets relative to the rate of interest charged on bank loans, and on the differential between the rates of interest on bank loans and alternative sources of funds.

The banking system seeks to ensure that there is a balance between the demand and supply of loanable funds both quantitatively and qualitatively. The quantitative balance requires that the total demand for loanable funds equals the total supply of such funds. The banking system also seeks a qualitative balance in the sense of matching the distribution of the term structures of their loans and deposits. The repayment period on bank loans varies from the very short term in the case of temporary transactions loans which are repaid within the current period, to the very long term in the case of loans to firms to finance investment projects.

Likewise, bank deposits vary with regard to the length of time which wealth holders are prepared to commit them. The banking system offers two general types of bank deposits. First there are current (or demand) accounts designed to act as temporary transactions balances. These accounts pay relatively low or zero rates of interest (or even negative rates of interest in the form of bank charges) but they can be used as a medium of exchange. Current accounts represent a very short-term commitment of wealth to the banking system. An alternative type of bank deposit are the deposit (or time or savings) accounts, which are designed as a means of holding wealth on a more long-term basis. These accounts offer relatively high rates of interest as a reward for the long-term commitment of funds to the banking system. There is likely to be a whole spectrum of deposit accounts on offer with the rates of interest rising with the length of the commitment of the funds.

The banking system can attempt to balance the distribution of the term structures of loans and deposits by varying the rates of interest payable. The imbalance created by the tendency for agents to wish to lend short but borrow long can be overcome, at least partially, by relating the rates of interest on loans and deposits with the length of the commitment of these funds. The relatively high rates of interest associated with the long-term commitment of funds should produce a counteracting tendency for agents to lend long but borrow short.

The banking system can manipulate the relative rates of interest on bank deposits and loans in order to achieve the qualitative balance in the distribution of the term structures of the commitment of funds. However, it cannot use the rate of interest to ensure the quantitative balance between the total demand for loanable funds and the total supply. The banking system is not a market for loanable funds in which the rate of interest acts as the price mechanism ensuring an allocative equilibrium. The demand and supply of loanable funds depends on a number of factors other than the rate of interest, principally the current rate of the monetary flow in the industrial sector. There is no reason whatsoever why the rate of the monetary flow in the industrial sector should adjust to ensure an allocative equilibrium in the banking system. The banking system is not characterized by the allocative mode of activity. Hence the demand-and-supply theory of price determination is not applicable to the determination of the rate of interest on loanable funds. It is more appropriate to treat the banking system as part of a monetary production economy in which the flow of funds to and from the banking system depends primarily on the rate of the aggregate monetary flow. The banking system should therefore be seen as within the utilization mode of activity.

The lack of a regulatory mechanism in the banking system creates the possibility that there may be insufficient demand for loanable funds relative to the available supply of loanable funds. The banking system may be faced with insufficient demand for new loans and too low a level of use of the credit facilities which it has extended to agents. This lack of demand for loanable funds is exacerbated by the operation of the credit multiplier. As new loans are used, this generates a new flow of funds into the banking system from the recipients of the loan-financed expenditure. The existence of an excess supply of loanable funds in the banking system creates the possibility of financial capital being underutilized. However, unlike industrial capital, there are alternative uses for financial capital beyond the provision of bank loans. If there is an excess supply of loanable funds, the banking system can shift these excess funds into the other forms of assets offered by the rest of the financial sector, thereby maintaining the full utilization of financial capital.

The stock-market system

Outside of the banking system the financial sector is made up of a series of stock markets. Within these stock markets, agents buy and sell real assets, equity and those traded forms of debt such as government bonds. There exists an individual market for each type of traded asset. The existence of these stock markets means that the capital values of traded assets can vary with market conditions, unlike bank deposits and loans. Thus there exists the potential for agents to make capital gains or losses on these traded assets. This can provide an alternative source of monetary return besides service payments.

The demand for a particular type of traded asset during the current period consists of two components:

1 The portfolio-adjustment demand from agents who wish to adjust the distribution of assets within their portfolios of wealth accumulated prior to the current period in favour of the particular asset.
2 The accumulation demand from agents who wish to increase the size of their portfolios by accumulating wealth from the current monetary flow.

The level of portfolio-adjustment demand for a particular type of traded asset depends on the total value of the previously accumulated stock of wealth and the propensity to allocate that stock of wealth to the particular asset. This propensity is likely to depend primarily on the rate of return of the particular asset relative to the rates of return of all other assets. If the current propensity is such that there is an insufficient quantity of the particular asset in the portfolios of one or more agents, this generates a demand for this particular asset.

The level of accumulation demand for a particular asset depends on the aggregate level of accumulation demand for all assets from the current flow of money income. Following the Keynesian behavioural assumptions, the aggregate accumulation demand is determined by the current rate of the monetary flow. The share of any particular asset of the aggregate accumulation demand depends on the outcome of the portfolio-adjustment process as determined by the relative rates of return of different assets. Thus the portfolio-adjustment demand for a particular type of traded asset depends on the portfolio decision, while the accumulation demand depends on the savings decision.

The supply of a particular type of traded asset during the current period consists of three components:

1 The portfolio-adjustment supply as agents adjust the distribution of assets within their portfolios of wealth accumulated prior to the current period away from the particular asset.
2 The asset-financed-expenditure supply as agents liquidate part of their existing stock of wealth in order to finance the purchase of currently produced goods and services.
3 The new-issue supply as agents offer new equity and traded debt during the current period to raise finance for expenditure on either currently produced goods and services or existing real and financial assets.

The level of portfolio-adjustment supply of a particular type of traded asset depends on the total value of the previously accumulated stock of wealth and the propensity to allocate that stock of wealth to the particular asset. This propensity is likely to depend primarily on the rate of return of the particular asset relative to the rates of return of all other assets. If the current propensity is such that there is an excess quantity of the particular asset in the portfolios of one or more agents, this generates a supply of this particular asset. The level of asset-financed expenditure supply of a particular asset depends on the aggregate level of such expenditure during the current period. Traditionally, the level of asset-financed expenditure is seen as depending on changes in the aggregate price level. The real value of the stock of wealth varies inversely with the aggregate price level. Thus as the aggregate price level falls, the real value of the stock of wealth rises. This is believed to lead, in turn, to an increase in expenditure on currently produced goods and services. This process is known as the Pigou effect. The share of such expenditure financed by the sale of a particular asset is a portfolio decision depending on the relative rates of return of all assets. The level of new-issue supply also depends on the aggregate level of demand for expenditure financed in this way. Following the Keynesian behavioural assumptions, it is likely that the aggregate level of consumption and investment expenditure financed in this way depends primarily on the current rate of monetary flow. The share of any particular asset in the aggregate level of current new issues is likely to depend on the costs (broadly defined) per unit of finance raised relative to other means of securing finance.

It follows, from the discussion above, that one of the principal determinants of both the demand for and supply of a particular type of traded asset is its rate of return relative to the rates of return of all other assets, *ceteris paribus*. The demand for a particular asset tends to rise as its relative rate of return rises, while the supply of that asset tends to fall. This reflects the desire of agents to increase the share of this asset within their portfolios overall. If the relative rate of return of an asset falls, this tends to lead to a fall in its demand but a rise in its supply as agents shift the distribution of their portfolios away from it.

The overall net rate of return from any asset is the sum of all the monetary and non-monetary returns from holding the asset discounted for risk. Within the monetary return, one element is the rate of service payment in the form of interest, dividends or rent. At any point during the current period, wealth holders possess the right to the service payment due in that period. The service payment is the reward to an agent from allowing others to have the use of a particular asset. This payment is fixed in absolute terms which may or may not vary over time. The rate of service payment is, by definition, the current absolute service payment per period as a percentage of the current market value of the asset. For those assets which are traded, the rate of service payment varies as the current market value of the asset varies. In particular, given the absolute service payment per period due to the wealth holder at any point in time, the rate of service payment varies inversely with the current market price of the particular asset. Inasmuch as the rate of service payment affects the overall net rate of return of an asset, it follows that there is an inverse relationship between current market price of an asset and its overall net rate of return, *ceteris paribus*.

Given the inverse relationship between the current market price and its rate of return, it follows that both the demand for and the supply of a particular asset varies with respect to the current market price of that asset, *ceteris paribus*. As the current market price of an asset rises, the demand for that asset falls since its rate of return has fallen. The supply of the asset is likely to rise. On the other hand, as the current market price of an asset falls, this tends to raise the demand for that asset but lower the supply. It follows, therefore, that in general there should exist a current market price for each traded asset such that there is market-clearing throughout the stock market system. This position of generalized market-clearing represents a perfect allocative equilibrium. It requires a perfectly atomistic structure and sufficient information in all stock markets. Thus the demand-and-supply theory of price determination can be used to provide an understanding of the operation of the stock-market system. The price mechanism acts as the means of regulation of the allocative process in the stock-market system.

It should be noted that the process by which the current market value of the stock of all traded assets is determined does not involve the whole of that stock. Rather, current market values are determined by that portion of the stock which agents are prepared to trade at any point in time. There may a number of factors other than price which determine the level of participation. There is no necessity why there should be participation in the stock markets by the whole of the stock of traded assets at any particular point in time, particularly if some assets are held for non-allocative reasons. Sentimental attachment to a particular specific type of asset is one such non-allocative influence which would result in the non-participation of a portion of the total stock of traded assets. Non-participation may also result because of the lack of information and the existence of significant transactions costs (including the costs involved in gathering relevant information). These barriers to participation are likely to be at their highest in the case of agents with relatively small stock holdings.

Speculation

The possibility of changes in the capital values of traded assets offers another type of monetary return from holding assets in addition to any service payments. The existence of the possibility of capital gains or losses creates the potential for speculation. Speculation occurs whenever agents acquire some 'news' which gives them reason to expect a change in the market prices of traded assets. Agents seek to generate profits by trading in advance of the expected movements in market prices. Agents may purchase assets in the expectation of an appreciation in their market value, or alternatively, agents may sell assets in order to avoid an expected fall in their market value.

Speculative activity in the stock market system falls into two classes: fundamentalist speculation and chartist speculation. Fundamentalist speculation occurs if agents believe that there is a divergence between the 'underlying' value of a particular asset and its current market value. If the agent expects there to be a corrective movement eventually in the market price of the asset towards its underlying value, this opens up the possibility of using this 'knowledge' advantageously by either buying in advance of an upward price correction or selling in advance of a downward price correction.

Chartist speculation occurs if agents believe that the current operation of the stock markets is such as to produce a movement in asset prices in a particular direction. Chartist speculation involves trying to chart the direction of the current momentum in the stock markets, making the appropriate trades in advance. Rather than comparing market prices with underlying values as the fundamentalist speculator does, the chartist is concerned with the market itself and the whole range of influences which may affect the future movement of market prices. The two types of speculation interact. Chartist speculation may attempt to 'ride on the back' of any significant generalized fundamentalist trading.

If sufficient agents speculate in the same way, speculation becomes a self-fulfilling prophecy. The trading which occurs as a result of speculative beliefs can bring about the actualization of the changes in market prices which were expected. For example, if sufficient agents believe, for whatever reason, that the market price of a particular asset will rise, this encourages these agents to increase their market demand for that asset. There will also be a tendency for the owners of the existing stock of the asset to maintain their holdings, thereby reducing the market supply of the asset. This increase in market demand for the asset coupled with the fall in its market supply will tend to result in an increase in the market price of the asset, the very expected movement which initiated the change. The increase in market price may, in turn, give rise to further speculative activity inasmuch as it leads to the expectation of further increases in the market price of the asset.

The nature of speculative activity is such that stock markets become prone to recurring booms and crashes. Stock markets can become locked into a cumulative causation process in which the market prices of traded assets continue to move upwards or downwards. If market prices are expected to rise, speculative activity can generate a self-reinforcing virtuous circle whereby speculation leads to the expected rise in market prices and, in so doing, fuels further speculation. Thus the stock market moves into a period of boom: a bull market prevails. On the other hand, if agents expect market prices to fall, speculation generates a vicious circle of decline in market prices in which the trading initiated by these pessimistic speculative beliefs brings about the actualization of the expected falls in market prices, generating further speculation and further falls in market prices. The stock markets moves into a period of crash: a bear market prevails.

The existence of speculation introduces a dynamic element into the allocative process within the stock-market system. At any point in time, the market prices of traded assets move towards their market-clearing levels. However, this allocative movement in market prices over time may create speculative beliefs as to the future movement of market prices. Thus, at any point in time, speculative beliefs about the future will affect the current levels of market demand and supply for an asset. Current market prices are, therefore, likely to be affected, at least partially, by past movements in prices, particularly those in the recent past, inasmuch as such past movements influence future expectations.

Equilibrium in the financial sector

A starting-point for the analysis of the behaviour of agents in the financial sector is the choice-theoretic approach of classical theory. Agents are assumed to optimize by seeking to maximize the overall net rate of return from their portfolios as a whole. This requires that every individual agent must equalize the overall net rate of return of each asset in their portfolio. If an agent does not equalize the overall net rate of return for each asset, this creates the possibility that the rate of return from the portfolio as a whole can be increased by adjusting the distribution of assets within the portfolio away from those assets with relatively low rates of return in favour of those assets with relatively high rates of return. The rate of return for a portfolio as a whole is only maximized once all opportunities for such profitable portfolio readjustment are exhausted.

The overall net rate of return for a particular asset is defined as the sum of all the monetary and non-monetary net returns which accrue from ownership of the asset, discounted for the risk associated with the asset. At any point in time the overall net rate of return can be expressed as:

$$x = r + k^e - v - l + g + u$$

where:

x is the overall net rate of return;
r is the rate of service payment;
k^e is the agent's expectation of the change in market price of the asset;
v is the agent's subjective evaluation of the risk attached to the asset;
l is the cost of convertibility into a means of exchange;
g is the net flow of any real services from an asset, allowing for such costs as depreciation, maintenance, and storage;
u is all other forms of utility gains and losses associated with ownership of the asset.

The following points should be noted about this definition:

1 All components of the overall net rate of return are expressed in their monetary equivalent for the current period as a percentage of the current market price of the asset.
2 The component v represents a numerical evaluation of the risk attached to a particular asset relative to all other assets. Thus v does not take account of any non-numerically quantifiable element of uncertainty attached to any particular asset relative to all other assets. Such uncertainty must be treated as an exogenous factor, assumed to be given for the purposes of analysis. The general state of uncertainty affecting all assets must also be treated in the same manner.
3 The components v and l together represent a measure of the illiquidity of an asset and are therefore a negative element within the overall net rate of return of an asset. By defini-

tion, money is a perfectly liquid asset with v and l both being zero.

4 The components g and u can be assumed to be fixed for the purposes of analysis, being determined by a variety of essentially non-economic factors.

In making their portfolio decisions, agents are faced with the choice of a whole range of types of assets. As has been argued above, one broad distinction in the range of assets available is between those assets which are traded within the stock-market system and those non-traded assets in the form of bank deposits offered by the banking system. Thus, from the very outset, it must be realized that agents are faced with a choice between assets whose rates of return are determined in very different ways because of the nature of the financial sector. Whereas the rates of return on traded assets are market-determined, the rates of return on bank deposits are managed by the institutions of the banking system themselves. These different processes of determination of the rates of return on assets interact since, ultimately, both types of assets are substitutes for each other within the portfolios of individual agents.

Turning first to bank deposits, the characteristics of this form of asset are such that the components k^e, v and g in the overall net rate of return are zero. If, in addition, it is assumed that the component u is also zero, it follows that:

$$x_i = r_i - l_i$$

where:

x_i is the overall net rate of return on the ith type of bank deposit;
r_i is the rate of interest on the ith type of bank deposit;
l_i is the cost of convertibility of the ith type of bank deposit.

The rate of interest on the ith type of bank deposit can, in turn, be considered to consist of the following two components:

$$r_i = r_{base} + d_i$$

where:

r_{base} is the base rate of interest set by the central bank;
d_i is the differential between the base rate of interest and the rate of interest on the ith type of bank deposit.

The central bank is the institution charged with the regulation of the banking system. One of its main instruments of regulation is the power to set the base rate of interest for the banking system. All other institutions within the banking system set their rates of interest on deposits and loans with reference to the base rate of interest. This can be viewed as the conductive determinant of the rate of interest on the ith type of bank deposit. The differential between the rate of interest on a particular type of bank deposit and the base rate, depends on a number of factors in much the same way as the pricing decision of firms within the industrial sector is affected by a number of different pressures. Banking institutions are likely to have a set of 'normal' differentials based on past experience. Banking institutions may depart from these 'normal' differentials as the result of allocative, strategic and positional considerations. For example, the whole set of differentials within the banking sytem may be adjusted as a result of the relationship between the aggregate demand for funds from the banking system and the aggregate supply of funds. Alternatively, individual banking institutions may have to alter their differentials because of the competitive pressures facing them within the process of strategic interaction between institutions competing for a share of the aggregate level of activity in the banking system.

The structure of the rates of interest on different types of bank deposits is mainly determined by the length of commitment of funds by depositors. The incremental rate of interest payable in return for long-term commitment of funds represents l_i, the cost of convertibility of these funds into a means of exchange inasmuch as this increment is lost if the funds are withdrawn on demand within the period of notice. Within any particular type of bank deposit, the rate of interest may vary with the size of the individual deposit.

The rate of interest on any particular type of bank loan is some 'normal' differential over the base rate of interest, adjusted for variations in the degree of risk and illiquidity between different types of bank loans. Again, the whole structure of such differentials across the banking system may be affected by allocative, strategic and positional pressures.

The regime under which the base rate of interest is set by the central bank is likely to take one of two possible forms. The first type of regime is the market regime whereby the central bank sets the base rate of interest with regard to the current allocative pressures within the financial sector. This can occur in one of two ways. First, the central bank may adjust the base rate of interest in response to any imbalance between the aggregate demand and supply of loanable funds in the banking system. Under this type of market regime, the base rate would be raised during times of excess demand for bank loans and lowered in times of excess supply. In effect, under this type of regime, the banking system would become a market for loanable funds with the base rate of interest acting as the means of allocative regulation. However, the effectiveness of the rate of interest as a price mechanism in this situation is severely limited by the fact that the aggregate demand and supply of loanable funds is not primarily determined by the rate of interest but rather depends on the rate of the monetary flow within the industrial sector. A second possible type of market regime is one in which the base rate is set with regard to movements in the rates of return on traded assets within the system of stock markets in the rest of the financial sector. Again, under this market regime, the base rate of interest acts as an allocative mechanism. In this case, the base rate is adjusted to ensure, at the very least, a tendency towards the equalization of the overall net rates of return between bank deposits and the traded forms of assets. These two types of market regime are not necessarily mutually exclusive and, indeed, may coincide inasmuch as the allocative pressures in the stock-market system determine the aggregate demand and supply of loanable funds in the banking system.

An alternative type of regime for the determination of the base rate of interest is the managed regime whereby the central bank sets the base rate of interest with regard to some set of policy objectives. Under this type of regime, the base rate of interest is not determined by the allocative processes within the financial sector. Rather, the base rate of interest becomes a macro policy instrument with which to influence the industrial sector. It is an indirect method of manipulation, relying for its effectiveness on the responsiveness of households and firms in the industrial sector to changes in the financial sector. Under this managed regime, the base rate of interest becomes a fixed parameter, acting as a constraint on the operation of the allocative processes within the financial sector.

The central bank can influence the financial sector in two ways other than the setting the base rate of interest. First, the central bank may set the liquidity ratio for the banking system by determining the proportion of a bank's assets which must be held in the form of liquid assets. This control over the liquidity ratio can be used by the central bank to affect the credit multiplier for the banking system as a whole. Second, the central bank can influence the financial sector through the buying and selling of government securities. The central bank is the most significant agent in the stock market system through its role as the government's broker. Such open market operations allow it to influence the market price of traded assets and thereby influence the portfolio decisions of individuals. The central bank can use its control of the liquidity ratio and/or open-market operations in conjunction with its control over the base rate of interest. For example, if the central bank operates a managed regime for the base rate of interest, it may use open-market operations to bring about changes in the stock-market system consistent with the change in the base rate of interest. Thus, if the central bank wishes to have a general reduction in the level of interest rates, it may reduce the base rate of interest and simultaneously decrease its net sales of government securities. The fall in the supply of government securities will tend to push up their market values and thereby reduce their rate of interest. The existence of open-market operations means that a central bank operating a market regime for the base rate of interest can have a *de facto* managed regime through the use of open-market operations to influence the stock-market system in order to bring about a desired change in the rates of interest.

The determination of the overall net rates of return on traded assets occurs within the stock-market system. Agents engage in a portfolio-allocation process to equalize the overall net rates of return from all assets in their portfolios. In the case of traded assets, this results in changes in the demand and supply of each type of traded assets with the current prices of traded assets moving towards their market-clearing levels. A perfect allocative equilibrium exists in the stock-market system if two conditions hold. First, there must be a system-level equilibrium in the sense of generalized market-clearing throughout the stock-market system. Second, there must also be an agent-level equilibrium in the sense of every agent achieving the equalization of the overall net rates of return for all assets in their portfolios.

For any individual agent, the overall net rate of return on a particular type of traded asset is primarily determined by the current market price of that asset and the current expectations of the agent about future movements in the market price. The overall net rate of return on a traded asset tends to be inversely related to the current market price of that asset. As has been discussed above, this is the result of service payments being fixed in nominal terms. As the market price of a traded asset rises, the fixed service payment is reduced as a percentage of that market price. As the market price falls, the rate of service payment rises. However, it cannot be concluded from this that there is an unambiguous inverse relationship between the current market price of an asset and the overall net rate or return. This is because changes in the current market price of an asset may.lead agents to adjust both their expectations of future capital gains and losses as well as their subjective evaluations of the risk attached to the particular asset. Inasmuch as agents believe that the current market price of an asset is at its expected level, any movement away from that price is likely to lead agents to adjust, in the opposite direction, their assessment of the risk attached to the asset and the expected future changes in its capital value. For example, a rise in the current market price above its expected level is likely to lead agents to revise downwards their expectations of future capital gains as well as to raise their assessment of the risk of future capital losses. Both these effects imply a reduction in the overall net rate of return, reinforcing the fall in the rate of service payment.

As has been argued above, the demand for a particular type of traded asset varies directly with its overall net rate of return, *ceteris paribus*, while its supply varies inversely. If there is an inverse relationship between the current market price of an asset and its overall net rate of return, it follows that there is likely to be a stable equilibrium level of market price such that the market demand and supply of the asset are equal.

The second principal determinant of the overall net rate of return of a particular type of traded asset are the expectations held by agents of the future changes in the capital value of the asset. These expectations are likely to depend in part on past changes in the market price of the asset to the extent that the agent forms expectations in an adaptive manner. In general, agents base their expectations on all pieces of information which they consider to be relevant. The information set on which agents form their expectations consists of information relating to a particular type of asset and information relating to the financial sector as a whole. If agents receive any piece of information which leads them to adjust their expectations of the overall net rate of return of one or more assets, this sets in motion a process of portfolio readjustment, leading to changes in the aggregate demand and supply of assets and, in the case of traded assets, to changes in the current market price.

Bank deposits and traded assets represent two substitute classes of assets with which agents can hold their wealth within their portfolios. It follows, therefore, that agents seek to equalize the overall net rate of return between these two classes of assets as well as between the different types within these two classes. However, the best portfolio allocation for the individual agent cannot be arrived at solely through a consideration of overall net rates of return in which all forms of assets are treated separately. This atomic assumption does not hold. Agents must also consider the organic properties arising from the nature of the portfolio as a whole. In particular, agents will wish to hold diversified portfolios in order to gain the advantages of risk spreading. Indeed, risk spreading is an important reason for holding bank deposits, despite their relatively low monetary rates of return.

If there is a change in the overall net rate of return associated with any particular type of asset, this leads to a portfolio readjustment process which may affect not only other assets of the same class, but also those of the other asset class. For example, if the central bank operates a managed regime for the base rate of interest, any change in the base rate results in the adjustment of the whole structure of interest rates on bank deposits and loans. This, in turn, implies that the relative overall net rates of return between bank deposits and traded assets has changed, setting off a portfolio readjustment process in which agents move out of those assets with the relatively low rates of return into those assets with the relatively high rates of return. Indeed, the change in the base rate of interest is likely to produce expectations of changes in the market prices of traded assets. These expectations will tend to bring about their own actualization to the extent that they generate speculative activity in the stock markets. This process of portfolio readjustment should eventually produce the re-establishment of the equalization of overall net rates of return across all assets.

If the portfolio readjustment process is initiated by a change in the overall net rate of return of one or more traded assets, this can lead to a change in the whole structure of interest rates on bank deposits and loans if the central bank operates a market regime for the base rate of interest which takes account of changes in the stock market system directly or indirectly through the spillover effect on the aggregate demand and supply of loanable funds to and from the banking system.

A perfect allocative equilibrium exists in the financial sector if all agents have optimized their wealth holdings such that the overall net rates of return are equalized across all assets in their portfolios. In such circumstances there is generalized market-clearing throughout the stock-market system with all agents able to fulfil their desired quantities of trade for all types of traded asset at the current level of market prices. There remains no scope for further profitable trades to take place. All such opportunities have been exploited.

The conditions for a perfect allocative equilibrium in which there is no incentive for agents to undertake further portfolio readjustment represents a position of long-run equilibrium. All agents expect current market prices to prevail in the future and these expectations are fulfilled. If expectations on market prices are fixed, there is no scope for speculative activity. Thus the notion of a long-run equilibrium is based on the twin assumptions that all agents are rational and have perfect information on which to base their expectations. This is the rational-expectations hypothesis in its strongest form. The position of long-run equilibrium only shifts if there are exogenous changes of which agents cannot have any prior expectations.

If the assumption of all agents having perfect information on endogenous influences on the future market prices of traded assets is relaxed, this has two implications. First, there is no longer a single set of expectations held by all agents; rather, there is a whole distribution of expectations. The behaviour of any individual agent depends on the information available to that agent and the particular methods of expectation formation adopted. The theoretical concept of a long-run equilibrium only remains useful in such circumstances if it is valid to reduce the whole distribution of expectations to a single set of expectations which are in some sense representative of the whole distribution.

The second effect of relaxing the informational assumption is to create the possibility of speculative activity. Speculation is all about the profitable use of the perceived informational advantages which agents believe themselves to possess. Speculation can only occur in the real world of imperfect information. The existence of imperfect information means that, in the short run, the portfolio readjustment process can be characterized as tending to produce a series of only temporary equilibria in which there is an equalization of rates of return with the implied generalized market-clearing in the stock market system but on the basis of expectations which are subsequently revised. To the degree that agents form their expectations adaptively by using past changes as an indicator of future changes, it follows that the movements in market prices involved in the current portfolio readjustment process can generate changes in the expectations of agents of future market prices. Such changes in expectations create the potential for profitable speculative trading, leading to further portfolio readjustments.

Even if there exists a long-run equilibrium associated with a representative set of expectations, it does not follow that the sequence of temporary short-run equilibria results in a stable adjustment process towards the long-run equilibria. Indeed, if there is significant chartist speculation within the stock market system, the result is likely to be a cumulative causation process in which market prices continue to move in a particular direction, either upwards or downwards. Initially, such speculation may either be generalized across all traded assets or restricted to particular types of traded assets. If the speculation is restricted to certain types of assets, this implies that the speculative pressure on market prices of those assets are completely dominating the allocative pressures created by the appearance of significant differences between the overall net rates of return of different assets. If such differences do appear, eventually allocative pressures assert themselves to produce a corrective adjustment towards the equalization of overall net rates of return. This correction may occur through the mechanism of expectations whereby the expectation of correction generates speculative activity which actualizes the correction. This allocative correction can result in one of two possible outcomes. First, the speculative activity can become generalized across all traded assets, with the market prices of other traded assets moving in the same direction as the market-leading assets. However, this corrective process can only become generalized across the whole of the financial sector if the central bank adopts a market regime for the determination of the base rate of interest. If the central bank does not adopt an accommodating strategy, this can act as an ultimate constraint on the continuation of generalized speculation, leading eventually to the reversal of the direction of movement of market prices of all traded assets.

The allocative correction does not necessarily take the form of generalized speculation. Alternatively, the correction can be achieved by a reversal in the direction of change of market prices of the particular assets involved before there are any significant spillover effects on other traded assets. In these circumstances, the speculative activity remains isolated, provided that there is a sufficient concentration of agents who expect a reversal in the direction of change. Such expectations bring about the actualization of the allocative correction.

The existence of imperfect information on the part of agents in the financial sector raises very severe doubts about the use of the choice-theoretic and equilibrium-theoretic approaches of classical theory. Without perfect information, the notion of optimal choice loses all operational content. The behaviour of agents becomes dependent on the specific nature of their information sets, the conventions and decision rules which they use and the learning procedures which they follow. Under these circumstances, the behavioural approach becomes a far more appropriate method of analysis. The choice-theoretic approach may come back into its own if it can be assumed that there is an efficient diffusion of information within the financial sector but, at best, the choice-theoretic approach will deal with just one aspect of behaviour in the financial sector. The inevitability of uncertainty about future outcomes means that agents will always rely on conventions to some degree or other. In particular, as Keynes pointed out, human beings tend to operate with regard to the principle of continuity, assuming the future to be like the recent past unless there is specific information to suggest otherwise.

The inadequacies of the choice-theoretic approach cast doubts on the validity of using the equilibrium-theoretic approach of classical theory. Under conditions of imperfect information the adjustment process depends on the specific learning procedures which agents adopt. It cannot be assumed that these learning procedures will result in an outcome associated with conditions of perfect information. Indeed, it is debatable as to whether or not equilibrium has much meaning under conditions of imperfect information. The concern is with trying to distinguish the processes of change, their magnitude and direction. Whether any process can be considered as tending towards some equilibrium point, will depend on agents maintaining their current patterns of behaviour. Such continuity in behaviour implies that agents consider the inevitable errors between their expectations and actual outcomes to be in some sense 'reasonable' under the circumstances. This requires agents to consider their errors to be random and within some acceptable bounds. If the errors are not considered to be 'reasonable' under the circumstances, this will result in a process of re-evaluation by agents of their behaviour patterns, involving various learning procedures. Inasmuch as this leads to changes in behaviour patterns, then processes of change will themselves be subject to change, as will the implied point of equilibrium.

The limitations of the choice-theoretic and equilibrium-theoretic approaches in the analysis of the financial sector coupled with the realization that the market-theoretic approach is inappropriate for an analysis of the banking system, lead to a very important point with regard to the use of classical theory for the analysis of the financial sector. Classical theory is but a useful starting-point for the analysis of the financial sector and can, by no means, be considered as a complete analysis. Classical theory provides one perspective, albeit one of much importance. But the financial sector must not be presupposed to be wholly within the allocative mode of activity. The banking system operates as part of monetary production economy, not an exchange economy. Furthermore, to presuppose only an allocative mode of activity is to abstract the analysis out from the pervasive uncertainty which characterizes behaviour in the financial sector as much as in the industrial sector. A proper consideration of the effects of uncertainty cannot be achieved by remaining within the classical frame of reference and its presupposition of perfect information and perfect foresight. Keynes was well aware of this in his analysis of the financial sector. The theory of liquidity preference may be a classical theory of allocation, but it is one which gives due consideration to the effects of uncertainty and the conventional behaviour which results.

A bootstraps theory of the rate of return

The portfolio decisions of agents in the financial sector generate a continual process of stock adjustment as agents seek to maximize the overall net rate of return from their holdings of wealth. The process results in the equalization of the overall net rate of return from all assets within the portfolios of agents. It is the tendency towards the equalization of overall net rates of return which represents the fundamental internal dynamic producing consistency within the financial sector. This internal dynamic operates primarily in the stock market system through movements in the market prices of traded assets. This can induce a change in the whole structure of interest rates in the banking system if the central bank operates under a market regime for setting the base rate of interest.

The internal dynamic created by the portfolio readjustment process explains the relationship between the overall net rates of return on all assets. What, therefore, determines changes in the level of the equilibrium overall net rate of return? To answer this, it must be remembered that this is a dynamic question. The equilibrium overall net rate of return at any point in time is the outcome of the whole preceding historical process. The concern is with the explanation of the direction and magnitude of the current propensity for change (or, indeed, with the explanation of why there may be no current propensity for change).

In explaining the dynamics of the equilibrium overall net rate of return, two of the most significant influences are (1) the nature of the expectations which agents hold and (2) the specific policy of the central bank with regard to the base rate of interest under a managed, non-market-determined, regime. Changes in either of these influences can set in motion a process of portfolio readjustment which can lead to a change in the equilibrium level of the overall net rate of return as a result of the movement towards the re-establishment of the equalization of the overall net rates of return across all assets. This is, quite intentionally, a bootstraps theory of the rate of return. There is no unique, objectively determined level for the equilibrium rate of return. It varies depending on past history and such current influences as the state of expectations. The notion of some unique, objectively determined equilibrium is the product of a deeply rooted attachment in Western thought to the twin, interrelated vices of static analysis and objective reductionism. The rate of return, as with so many economic variables, results from a continuous dynamic process of interaction, influenced by, and inseparable from, past experience. Patterns of economic behaviour produce adjustment processes as agents seek to achieve consistency between what may be conflicting and contradictory influences. This search for consistency creates a bootstraps property in which there are no exogenous factors exercising some primary influence in determining the eventual outcome. The assumption of exogeneity is an arbitrary one, used purely for the purposes of analytical convenience. Too often the reductionist presupposition underlying many theoretical systems has led to the construction of very rigid hierarchies of cause-and-effect relationships with one particular factor or set of factors being vested with an all-powerful primacy in the chains of causation. Such hierarchical theoretical structures blind their followers to the dynamic and interactive nature of processes of change in which no factor or single set of factors have any primacy whatsoever.

The nature of the financial sector: a summary

At any point in time the stock of wealth within the financial sector consists of wealth accumulated prior to the current period plus the net inflow from the monetary flow in the current period. This current inflow, in turn, consists of a transactions demand and an asset demand, the latter demand resulting from the savings decisions of agents. On the Keynesian behavioural assumptions, the propensity to save out of the current flow of money income depends primarily on the current rate of flow of money income. Given the stock of wealth at any point in time, agents face the portfolio decision of how to allocate this stock of wealth between the different types of assets available. This is an allocative problem. Rational agents optimize their portfolios by equating the overall net rate of return of every type of asset in their portfolios, giving due consideration to the risk-spreading properties of the portfolio as a whole. In allocating their financial capital, agents do not face any utilization problem as with industrial capital.

Financial capital is used to store wealth and, since such capital must always be held in some form or other, it follows that financial capital is always fully utilized.

The nature of the financial sector is such that the allocative process operates through two very different systems. The financial sector consists of the banking system and the stock-market system. These two systems offer different forms of assets. The banking system offers bank deposits, a non-traded form of asset which are highly liquid and on which a rate of interest may be earned. The stock-market system, on the other hand, offers a range of traded assets which are less liquid but on which higher monetary rewards may be gained through service payments and the potential for capital gains. Bank deposits tend to be appropriate for transactions balances and short-term savings where the needs of convertibility into a means of exchange are important. Bank deposits also offer a very low risk means of storing wealth. Traded assets are more appropriate for longer-term savings, where the needs of capital growth are important rather than convertibility.

The stock-market system is made up of a series of markets in which different types of assets are traded. At any point in time the price of a particular asset tends towards the equilibrium level at which the quantity demanded equals the quantity supplied. Thus the system operates in the manner of an exchange economy. Agents operate within the allocative mode of activity in the sense that their individual allocative decisions are regulated, in aggregate, by the price mechanism within a series of interdependent markets. Thus the classical frame of reference offers an appropriate starting-point for understanding the operation of the stock-market system. The demand-and-supply theory of price determination is applicable to the explanation of how the market prices of traded assets are determined. But classical theory, it must be remembered, is only a starting-point, no more.

From the initial perspective of the classical frame of reference, the price mechanism operates within the stock-market system as an invisible hand, ensuring a tendency towards generalized market-clearing. This is a position of long-run equilibrium if, for all agents, the overall net rate of return is equalized across all types of assets, both traded and non-traded, and there are no expectations of further changes in market prices. In the short run, however, the allocative process within the stock-market system is, in part, influenced by speculative trading created by the potential for capital gains and losses on wealth held in the form of traded assets. The existence of significant speculative activity creates the potential for booms and crashes in the market prices of traded assets. Speculation is one example of the more general point that imperfect information and uncertainty create a context of behaviour that is not purely allocative and hence not amenable to analysis by the classical approach only.

The other component of the financial sector is the banking system, consisting of banks and other similar institutions which operate as the intermediaries in the non-market transfer of loanable funds. There is no market for loanable funds in the banking system. The stock of bank deposits and outstanding bank loans accumulated prior to the current period is determined by the historical process, while the current increments in the quantities of bank funds which are demanded and supplied by agents are determined, primarily, by the current rate of monetary flow within the industrial sector. Thus the aggregate quantities of bank funds which are demanded and supplied at any point in time are likely to be relatively price-insensitive. Furthermore, to the degree that the central bank adopts a managed regime to the base rate of interest on which the whole structure of interest rates within the banking system depends, the rates of interest on bank funds do not adjust in response to any imbalance between the demand and supply of bank funds. Indeed, there is no economic compulsion for individual institutions or the banking system as a whole to ensure equality between demand and supply. Any imbalance in the banking system as a whole only results in a net flow of funds between the banking system and the stock-market system. Thus, for example, if the banking system is unable to achieve its desired level of lending, given its stock of deposits, this underutilization problem can be resolved by the transfer of these excess funds to the stock market system through the purchase of traded assets.

The operation of the banking system does not therefore fall within the allocative mode of activity. The rates of interest on bank funds do not act as a price mechanism to ensure the equality of demand and supply. The banking system does not operate as an exchange economy, even though the portfolio decisions of agents involves the allocation of their stocks of wealth between the alternative forms of asset offered by the banking system and the stock-market system. Since, within the banking system, this process is not regulated by the price mechanism operating in a series of markets, it cannot be considered to be within the allocative mode of activity. In fact, the operation of the banking system is more properly considered as within the utilization mode of activity that prevails in a monetary production economy. The level of utilization of bank funds as a supply of loanable funds is not regulated by a price mechanism but depends on the rate of the monetary flow. Inasmuch as there is an excess supply of bank funds, the actual level of bank lending becomes entirely demand-determined.

The operation of the banking system renders the money supply an endogenously, demand-determined variable. Bank funds are money by virtue of their liquidity. The process of transfer of these funds through lending creates further liquidity by providing borrowers with the means to finance expenditure. As these borrowed funds are used, a circular process occurs whereby bank loans which are spent become an income to other agents who may, in turn, deposit part of these funds with the banking system. This is the credit multiplier process. Thus the quantity of bank funds at any point in time is ultimately determined by those factors which influence the level of demand for bank funds. It is pure mythology to treat the money supply as some exogenously given magnitude. Such is not the nature of money in the modern capitalist economy.

It should be remembered that the discussion in the present analysis is wholly within the abstract theoretical mode of discourse. In particular, the definitions of the banking system and the stock-market system are definitions based on the present theoretical analysis. These two systems are identified as spheres of utilization and allocative modes of activity, respectively. These theoretical definitions have not taken into account any empirically based considerations drawing on the specific institutional features of one or more actual cases. Such empirical concerns are crucially important, and the definitions will need to be adjusted accordingly as the theoretical analysis is applied to specific empirical cases. One problem likely to arise is the fact that in many cases banks are institutions which operate in the stock market system as well as the banking system. Thus, for example, within actual banking systems there are inter-bank markets for trading bank deposits which facilitate the process of matching up the demand for loans and the supply of bank deposits when there is a multi-bank system. These inter-bank markets may mean that the theoretical boundaries between the banking system and the stock market system are not clearly distinguished empirically. The one-to-one relationship between institutions and modes of activity breaks down when actual cases are examined. Despite these empirical problems, however, the distinction between the two very different modes of behaviour remains relevant for any analysis of the financial sector.

Classical and Keynesian theories of the financial sector revisited

The above analysis of the financial sector can be seen as an extension of earlier classical and Keynesian theories. Both the classical theories and the Keynesian theories of the financial sector can be characterized in terms of a set of six basic propositions. The Keynesian set represent partly a generalization of some of the classical propositions, and partly the rejection of others. The synthesis of both theories which emerges, in the light of the Keynesian critique, forms the foundation of the present analysis of the financial sector.

The classical theories of the financial sector consist of the following six basic propositions:

Proposition C1:   The only relevant asset is money.
Proposition C2:   The money supply is an exogenously determined variable.
Proposition C3:   Money is demanded solely for transactions purposes.
Proposition C3a: Money is demanded for both transactions and non-transactions purposes with a fixed proportional relationship between the two types of demands.

Together, propositions C1 to C3 provide the basis of the quantity theory of money in which the aggregate price level acts as the allocative mechanism which ensures equality between the demand and supply of money. Proposition C3a is a later version of proposition C3, developed in the light of Keynesian arguments for the existence of non-transactions demands for money (see proposition K1 below). Proposition C3a renders these Keynesian arguments consistent with the quantity theory of money.

Proposition C4:   The supply of loanable funds through savings is an allocative decision between current consumption and future consumption determined by the rate of interest.

Proposition C5:   The rates of flow of loanable funds to and from the financial sector are brought into equality through the operation of the rate of interest.

Propositions C4 and C5 provide the basis of the loanable funds theory of the rate of interest in which the rate of interest acts as the allocative mechanism which ensures that there is equality between investment and savings, which represent, respectively, the demand for, and the supply of, loanable funds.

Proposition C6:   The allocative decision between current consumption and future consumption with regard to the accumulated stock of wealth is determined by the aggregate price level.

Proposition C6 represents the so-called real balance or wealth effect, a later development in classical theory in response to the emergence of Keynesian arguments for the deficiency of aggregate demand.

The Keynesian theories of the financial sector consist of the following six propositions:

Proposition K1:   In addition to the demand for balances for transactions purposes, there is also an asset demand for balances as a means of storing wealth.

Proposition K1 represents a generalization of the classical proposition C3 which limited consideration solely to the transactions demand for balances.

Proposition K2:   There are two types of assets, money and bonds.

Proposition K2 represents the generalization of the classical proposition C1 to allow for assets other than money, with different attributes. In particular, bonds are less liquid than money but earn a rate of interest. This creates the possibility of an allocative trade-off by agents between the degree of liquidity and the rate of interest.

Proposition K3: The portfolio decision by an agent on whether to hold money or bonds is an allocative decision determined by the rate of interest.

Proposition K3 follows from the assumption of rationality on the part of agents who face the allocative trade-off implied by proposition K1 and K2.

Proposition K4: The levels of demand and supply in the markets for money and bonds are brought into equality by adjustments in the rate of interest.

Taken together, the proposition K1 to K4 provide the basis of the Keynesian theory of liquidity preference in which the rate of interest acts as the allocative mechanism, ensuring a tendency towards generalized market-clearing within the financial markets. The Keynesian theory of liquidity preference represents the rejection of both the quantity theory of money and the loanable funds theory as theories of the allocative processes operating within the financial sector.

Proposition K5: The savings decision by an agent is not an allocative decision determined by the rate of interest.

Proposition K5 follows from the behavioural assumptions underlying the Keynesian consumption function in which the level of consumption and savings are determined primarily by the current rate of flow of money income. This is a non-allocative process and implies the rejection of the classical proposition C4.

Proposition K6: The money supply in an endogenously determined variable.

Proposition K6 is a later development in Keynesian theory in response to the revival of the quantity theory of money in the more modern form of monetarism. The notion that the money supply is primarily demand-determined implies the rejection of the classical proposition C2, one of the necessary foundations of the quantity theory of money.

The current analysis of the financial sector is an extension of this classical–Keynesian synthesis on the nature of the financial sector. With regard to Keynes's own generalization of the classical theories of the financial sector, the current analysis moves beyond it only to the extent of highlighting the differences in the modes of operation of the banking system and the stock market system, as well as the endogeneity of the money supply. Both of these developments are in the spirit of Keynes if not in fact contained, at least implicitly, in his own writings. Whether such a statement of interpretation is a fair representation of how Keynes himself viewed these matters is an academic question for the historians of economic thought to debate. The important point is the assertion that the view of the financial sector contained in the current analysis, inspired in part by a reading of Keynes's *General Theory*, provides an acceptable understanding of how the financial sector in the modern capitalist economy actually operates. In this respect the question of validity or otherwise of the implied interpretation of Keynes is entirely irrelevant.

The interaction of the industrial and financial sectors: a preliminary view

The classical approach

The classical analysis of the interaction between the industrial and financial sectors is provided by the theory of the loanable funds market. The rate of interest acts as the price mechanism within the loanable funds market ensuring that the demand for loanable funds for investment purposes equals the supply of loanable funds from savings. Market-clearing in the loanable funds market ensures that there is sufficient aggregate demand in the industrial sector to support a full-employment level of output.

The theory of the loanable funds market implies that there is no conflict between the industrial sector and the financial sector.

The rate of interest reconciles the needs of both sectors since equilibrium in the loanable funds market in the financial sector implies simultaneously that there is equilibrium in the goods market in the industrial sector. This convergence between the needs of the industrial and financial sectors follows from the classical belief that the capitalist economy is an exchange economy in which all economic activity is allocative, being regulated by the price mechanism within a system of interdependent markets. This unitary view of the nature of the capitalist economy creates the possibility that there is a particular set of prices which can ensure generalized market-clearing. This position of general equilibrium implies the reconciliation of the interests of all agents, be they in the industrial sector or the financial sector. This is the essential message of the invisible-hand theorem of classical theory.

Later classical theories further strengthened the notion that there is a convergence of interest between the industrial and financial sectors by postulating the existence of the wealth effect. The wealth effect relates to changes in the level of aggregate demand resulting from the changes in the real value of the stock of wealth caused by changes in the aggregate price level. The wealth effect can overcome any interest rate maladjustment implied by the Keynesian theory of liquidity preference which recognized that the rate of interest played an allocative role with respect to the money market in addition to any allocative role within the loanable funds market. The introduction of the wealth effect implies that there is a dual allocative mechanism consisting of the rate of interest and the aggregate price level which regulates the interaction between the industrial and financial sectors to ensure that there is sufficient aggregate demand within the industrial sector.

Classical theory also highlights the role of money wages in bringing about a convergence between the two sectors. According to the quantity theory of money, the aggregate price level acts as the allocative mechanism within the money market in the financial sector, ensuring that the demand for money equals the exogenously determined supply of money. On the other hand, the level of output in the industrial sector is determined in the labour market. Within the labour market the real wage acts as the allocative mechanism, ensuring that there is a tendency towards a full-employment equilibrium, with the demand for labour equal to the supply of labour. In order for there to be equilibrium simultaneously in both the money market in the financial sector and the labour market in the industrial sector, the wage bargain must set the money wage such that, given the equilibrium aggregate price level determined in the money market, the implied real wage is at the market-clearing level. If labour bargains for too high a money wage, given conditions in the money market, the result is a below-full-employment level of output in the industrial sector.

The classical theory of the loanable funds market implies a particular relationship between the rate of interest on loanable funds and the rate of profit in the industrial sector. The rate of interest on loanable funds is equal to the rate of profit on the marginal investment project undertaken by industrial firms. In other words, the rate of interest equals the marginal physical productivity of the stock of industrial capital. The average rate of profit exceeds the rate of interest to the extent that the average physical productivity of the existing stock of industrial capital exceeds the productivity of the marginal increment to that stock. This marginal productivity theory of the rate of interest implies that the rate of interest is a real variable, reflecting the technical conditions of production. The equilibrium rate of interest set in the loanable funds market is that rate of interest which equates the marginal physical productivity of the stock of industrial capital with the marginal rate of time preference for savers between current and future consumption.

Beyond the classical approach: a first step

The present analysis has attempted to move beyond classical theory by recognizing that the industrial and financial sectors operate in very different ways. It has been argued above that the capitalist economy is not an exchange economy in which the price mechanism regulates all economic activity. Thus it follows that the invisible-hand theorem of classical theory is not applicable to the capitalist economy. It is possible that there may be no convergence between the interests of the industrial and financial sectors. Indeed, far from there being any convergence in the needs of the two sectors, their interaction is likely to be characterized by inevitable conflicts, particularly, as is discussed more fully in chapter 6, with regard to their policy demands of the central authorities.

The essence of the present analysis is Keynes's contention that the industrial sector does not operate within the allocative mode of activity. This implies that there is no loanable funds market in which the rate of interest equates investment and savings. Rather, the flow of funds to and from the industrial and financial sectors is regulated by the multiplier process. It is the rate of the current monetary flow within the industrial sector which adjusts to ensure that there is no net flow of funds between the two sectors. This raises the possibility that the industrial sector may have to operate at a level of output below the full-employment one in order to maintain the balance in the flow of funds between the two sectors. The industrial sector bears the brunt of the automatic adjustment process.

The rate of interest does not bring about the convergence of the industrial and financial sectors through a loanable funds market. Rather, the rate of interest is determined within the financial sector in the portfolio adjustment process as agents seek to equalize the overall net rates of return across all forms of assets in which the stock of financial capital may be held. This process involves the whole of the accumulated stock of financial capital, not just the current incremental inflows and outflows. The determination of the whole structure of interest rates on bank funds depends on the regime adopted by the central bank for setting the base rate of interest. If a market regime is adopted, the base rate of interest is determined solely by the stock adjustment process within the financial sector. The base rate is only set with any regard for the needs of the industrial sector if a managed regime is adopted with the appropriate policy objectives.

Thus the capitalist economy at the macro level can be considered to exhibit two principal but very different modes of activity: the allocative mode of activity and the utilization mode of activity. The allocative mode of activity is the stock adjustment process as regulated by the price mechanism within a market. The utilization mode of activity refers to the flow utilization process as regulated by the multiplier mechanism through adjustments in the rate of the monetary flow. The existence of these two different modes of activity creates the Capitalist Dichotomy, a unique feature of the capitalist economy. The Capitalist Dichotomy refers to the separation at the macro level between the arena of the allocative mode of activity and the arena of the utilization mode of activity. In the macro capitalist economy it is the stock market system in the financial sector which is the arena of the allocative mode of activity. The arena of the utilization mode of activity is the industrial sector and the banking system. Thus the industrial sector and the banking system. Thus the interface between these two arenas lies within the financial sector. It is at this interface that the exchange economy and the monetary production economy interconnect.

The differences in the modes of activity in the industrial and financial sectors create a sequential process within the capitalist economy in which the operation of the financial sector dominates, to the degree that the rates of interest on bank loans and traded forms of debt are set by the financial sector alone in isolation of the needs of the industrial sector. These rates of interest are likely to affect the current rates of flow of funds between the two sectors, leading to a multiplier process in which the rate of the current monetary flow in the industrial sector adjusts. If the financial sector generates a rise in interest rates which lowers the rate of inflow of funds to the industrial sector relative to the rate of outflow, this induces a reduction in the rate of the current monetary flow within the industrial sector which may result in a lower rate of output flow with an associated lower level of employment.

The operation of the financial sector is such that its own internal dynamic determines the rates of return on assets. This is the bootstraps property of the financial sector. One implication of this is that the rate of profit is no longer a real variable related to the technological conditions of production (although, outside the short-run context of the present analysis, it is likely that the rate of profit may influence changes in such technological conditions). The rate of profit is the current rate of flow of monetary profits relative to the value of the industrial capital used to generate that flow. The current rate of flow of monetary profits depends on the conditions within the industrial sector. In particular, there is likely to be a positive relationship between the absolute level of monetary profits and the level of utilization of the industrial capital stock, which, in turn, is likely to be positively related to the current rate of the monetary flow. However, inasmuch as the ownership of the industrial capital stock takes the form of equity which is traded, it follows that the value of the industrial capital stock depends on the market price of equities as determined by the market forces of demand and supply. Thus the market price of equities depends not only on the past, current and expected performances of industrial capital, but also on the behaviour of the financial sector as a whole. It follows, therefore, that the rate of profit on industrial capital is determined as the result of the interaction of factors within the industrial and financial sectors. It is incorrect and misleading to consider the rate of profit as a real variable which in some way reflects the marginal physical productivity of the industrial capital stock. This is yet another of those widely held theoretical myths to which classical theory has taught blind acceptance.

The recognition that the rate of profit depends on factors in both the industrial and the financial sectors can have important implications for the operation of industrial capital. For example, it is widely accepted that the equity ownership of the industrial capital stock has led to the separation of ownership and control within modern industrial firms. Ownership rests in the hands of those financial agents who hold the stock of equity, whereas control of the industrial capital stock lies with the management within industrial firms. It may be supposed that this separation of ownership and control leads to a neat separation in the objectives of equity owners and the management of industrial firms with regard to the constituent components of the rate of profit. The management within industrial firms could be considered to be concerned with the absolute rate of flow of monetary profits as determined by conditions within the industrial sector. The owners of industrial capital, on the other hand, could be considered to be concerned with the market price of the equity stock as determined by conditions within the financial sector. However, this separation of interest breaks down if the management within industrial firms pursue any objectives relating to the market price of the equity stock. This may occur through the need to achieve a certain rate of profit in order to attract external funding from the financial sector. Alternatively, the management of industrial firms may seek to maintain the market price of their equity above that level which may lead to the threat of takeover. Such concerns lead to the financialization of industrial capital whereby the behaviour of the management of industrial firms is influenced by industrial and financial objectives, with the possibility that the financial objectives may take prominence. For example, the level of investment by industrial firms may be reduced if the desire to maintain a high market price for their equity leads the management of industrial firms to raise the level of dividends at the expense of retained earnings for investment purposes. The financialization of industrial capital can also lead the industrial sector to adopt a shorter-term time horizon in its choice of actions in which the concern is to achieve short-term financial objectives rather than the longer-term industrial objectives of growth through investment.

The industrial and financial sectors also interact through the policy actions of the central authorities. If the central authorities attempt to manage the aggregate performance of the industrial sector, the policies adopted may have a spillover effect on the financial sector. For example, the central authorities may attempt to increase the level of activity within the industrial sector by a debt-financed fiscal expansion. The increase in the supply of this type of traded asset tends to induce a downward adjustment in the market prices of traded assets. Alternatively, the central authorities can attempt to manage the industrial sector indirectly by means of monetary policies directed at the financial sector which actively seek to generate positive spillover effects to the industrial sector. However, if the central bank sets the base rate of interest using either a market regime or a managed regime with inappropriate policy objectives, this can result in negative spillover effects for the industrial sector.

The interaction between industrial and financial sectors through the policies of the central authorities need not involve the actual implementation of these policies. If the performance of either sector gives rise to expectations of a particular policy response on the part of financial agents, the speculative activity to which this may give rise can set off a chain reaction with spillover effects on the industrial sector. For example, if there is a significant increase in the level of unemployment in the industrial sector, this can lead to agents in the financial sector expecting a debt-financed fiscal expansion. Such expectations can lead to a fall in the market prices of the existing stock of such debt instruments as agents seek to avoid the capital losses expected to result from the expansion. To the extent that this speculative activity leads to an increase in the level of interest rates, this may lead to a fall in investment and hence further increases in the level of unemployment, with the obvious effects on the expectations of agents in the financial sector. Thus a cumulative process of decline is set off in the industrial sector with the momentum provided by the financial sector.

6

Unemployment and Inflation

Unemployment

Classical theories of unemployment

Classical theory presupposes that the capitalist economy is an exchange economy in which all economic behaviour falls within the allocative mode of activity. This means that all economic relationships are considered to consist of the exchange of commodities within markets, regulated by the price mechanism. Thus classical theory sees the employment relationship between firms and households as the exchange of a stock of labour services. This exchange occurs within the labour market, which constitutes the supply side of the economy. Both the demand for labour by firms and the supply of labour by households is deemed to depend on the real wage. If the labour market is perfectly competitive and all agents possess sufficient information, the real wage acts as the price mechanism in the manner described by the classical demand-and-supply theory of price determination. Thus classical theory derives the theoretical result that the capitalist economy automatically adjusts towards a market-clearing (i.e. full employment) level of output on the supply side, provided there are no structural and informational imperfections in the economic system. This particular application of the invisible-hand theorem is one of the most influential results produced by economic theory. It is especially significant at the current point in time in the history of capitalist economies when again it holds sway over the minds of most policy-makers.

Unemployment exists whenever a part of the potential labour force within an economy is either unwilling to actively seek employment or unable to find employment. The part of the potential labour force which is unwilling to seek employment is defined as voluntary unemployment. The part of the potential labour force which is unable to find employment is defined as frictional unemployment. Classical theories of unemployment are theories of voluntary and frictional unemployment since, ultimately, these are the only forms of unemployment which can exist in an exchange economy. The classical frame of reference does not allow for any other forms of unemployment. Classical theory treats the phenomenon of unemployment as a problem of misallocation. Thus classical theory has developed a whole array of imperfectionist theories of unemployment which explain unemployment as the result of structural and informational imperfections within the economy. These imperfections can cause unemployment either directly or indirectly. If the imperfections are located in the labour market, they can cause unemployment directly by reducing the potential level of employment generated on the supply side. Unemployment can also be caused indirectly if structural and informational imperfections on the demand side lead to a breakdown of Say's Law such that there is insufficient aggregate demand to maintain the potential level of employment determined by forces on the supply side.

Frictional unemployment occurs whenever some of those who are actively seeking employment are unable to find employment. This can be caused by changes in the distribution of the aggregate level of employment between individual products, firms and industries, between geographical locations as well as between different skills. These changes may be short run in nature, as in the case of seasonal unemployment, or the result of more longer-run factors, as in the case of structural unemployment arising from shifts in resources between industries. These can be considered as dynamic frictions. An alternative form of frictional unemployment is that caused by informational frictions in the form of imperfections within the information sets of agents. These informational imperfections can occur either in the quantity-offer information set of agents or in their price-adjustment information set. Quantity-offer information refers to the information required by an agent in order to determine the optimal quantity to trade of a particular commodity given the market conditions. Price-adjustment information, on the other hand, refers to the information required by price-setters in order to determine the optimal level of price for a particular commodity given the market conditions.

Informational imperfections may exist either on the supply side, resulting in direct frictional unemployment, or on the demand side, resulting in indirect frictional unemployment. The distinction between direct and indirect with regard to unemployment caused by informational imperfections needs some clarification because of the complications created by the composite nature of the real wage, the relevant price variable in the labour market. The real wage is made up of two elements: the money wage and the aggregate price level. The money wage, determined as it is within the wage bargain, is a supply side variable, but the aggregate price level should properly be considered a demand side variable, determined as it is in the goods and money markets. Thus, if unemployment arises from imperfect quantity-offer and price-adjustment information with regard to the money wage, this should be viewed as direct frictional unemployment. One type of direct frictional unemployment is the search unemployment which results from the reduction in the effective supply of labour as households search for quantity-offer information on the distribution of wage offers. The unemployment which arises from imperfect quantity-offer and price-adjustment information with regard to the aggregate price level, should be viewed as indirect frictional unemployment.

Voluntary unemployment occurs whenever a part of the potential labour force does not actively seek employment. The difference between the potential labour force and the actual supply of labour reflects the participation rate of labour which is determined by a number of economic and non-economic factors. Inasmuch as the decision to participate within the labour market is made on the basis of a rational allocative choice between work and leisure, the main economic determinant of the actual supply of labour is likely to be the level of the real wage (after tax), given the level of wealth and other sources of unearned income such as unemployment benefits. Following Keynes, however, it is convenient to also include, under the category of voluntary unemployment, all of that unemployment created by structural imperfections within the economy. The presence of significant concentrations of monopoly power on either the demand side or the supply side can lead to a reduction in the aggregate level of output and employment as a result of the rational allocative choices made by those agents with monopoly power. The unemployment which occurs is voluntary in the sense of being the result of voluntary choices by those with monopoly power, even though the unemployment which occurs may be an involuntary outcome from the point of view of those 'outsiders' who have no monopoly power. Voluntary unemployment caused by structural imperfections can be classified as direct or indirect, depending on whether the structural imperfections are located on the supply side or the demand side, respectively.

Classical theory believes that the level of unemployment within a capitalist economy tends towards the natural rate of unemployment. The natural rate of unemployment is the equilibrium rate of unemployment which is associated with full employment. The natural rate of unemployment is made up of four components:

1 Voluntary unemployment due to non-participation. This is the level of unemployment which arises from the decision on the part of some households not to participate in the labour market when the real wage is at the market-clearing level, under conditions of perfectly competitive markets on both the supply side and the demand side of the economy.
2 Voluntary unemployment due to structural imperfections. This is the level of unemployment which results from the presence of monopoly power on the supply side and/or the demand side.
3 Frictional unemployment due to dynamic frictions.
4 Frictional unemployment due to imperfect quantity-offer information on the equilibrium money wage (as determined by the degree of structural imperfection).

Thus the natural rate of unemployment is the level of unemployment which is associated with the absence of all forms of indirect frictional unemployment resulting from informational imperfections as well as the absence of those particular forms of direct frictional unemployment which result from either imperfect price-adjustment information with regard to the money wage or imperfect quantity-offer information generated by any disequilibrium process of adjustment in the money wage. In other words, the natural rate of unemployment is the level of unemployment in an economy which satisfies the following three conditions:

1 There is no deficiency of aggregate demand as the result of informational imperfections.
2 All agents have perfect information on the aggregate price level.
3 The money wage has fully adjusted, taking into account any structural imperfections which exist.

It follows from the notion of the natural rate of unemployment that the central authorities can reduce the natural rate by adopting micro-focused policies designed to combat the underlying causes of each of the four components of the natural rate. Voluntary unemployment due to non-participation can be reduced by increasing the economic incentives to work through, for example, changes in tax allowances and unemployment benefits. Voluntary unemployment due to structural imperfections can be reduced by limiting the degree of monopoly power in the economy through, for example, constraints on the actions of trade unions. Frictional unemployment due to dynamic frictions can be reduced by measures designed to increase the dynamic efficiency of the labour market. The provision of retraining schemes and mobility allowances are examples of this type of policy. Finally, frictional unemployment due to imperfect quantity-offer information on the equilibrium money wage can be reduced through measures designed to improve the flow of information within the labour market.

Disequilibrium unemployment occurs whenever the economy diverges away from the natural rate of unemployment. Disequilibrium unemployment is made up of different types of frictional unemployment. There are four types of disequilibrium unemployment which can be distinguished:

1 Direct frictional unemployment due to imperfect price-adjustment information with regard to the money wage.
2 Direct frictional unemployment due to imperfect quantity-offer information generated by any disequilibrium process of adjustment with regard to the money wage.
3 Indirect frictional unemployment due to imperfect quantity-offer information with regard to the aggregate price level.
4 Indirect frictional unemployment due to a deficiency in aggregate demand resulting from factors other than structural imperfections on the demand side.

The debate between the neoclassical/monetarist and classical Keynesian schools of thought within classical theory has centred on the significance and causes of these different types of disequilibrium unemployment. The characteristic belief of the neoclassical/monetarist school is that there is sufficient price-adjustment information within the economy to ensure market-clearing. Thus the neoclassical/monetarist school has tended to develop theories of unemployment which highlight the effects of imperfect quantity-offer information. These theories are known collectively as the 'new microeconomics'. Two of the most important of these theories are the search theories of unemployment and the theory of the expectations-augmented Phillips curve. Search theories can explain the direct frictional unemployment created by any disequilibrium process of adjustment in the money wage. Changes in the money wage can generate unemployment as agents quit their current employment and extend the duration of any period of unemployment in order to search for quantity-offer information on the changes in the general distribution of wage offers implied by changes in specific wage offers. The theory of the expectations-augmented Phillips curve explains how changes in the level of indirect frictional unemployment can occur as the result of firms and households in the labour market having to bargain on the basis of their own expectations of the future rate of inflation during the period over which the currently determined money wage will remain fixed.

The characteristic belief of all Keynesian schools of thought is that the main cause of unemployment is the deficiency of aggregate demand consequent on the operation of the multiplier process. However, the search for the microfoundations which underlie Keynesian macro analysis has been dominated by those who have interpreted Keynes's *General Theory* from the perspective of the classical frame of reference. It is this classical interpretation of Keynes which has been developed by the classical Keynesian school of thought. The inevitable result of the classical Keynesian approach has been the development of imperfectionist theories of unemployment. In particular, recent classical Keynesian theories have provided theories of disequilibrium types of frictional unemployment, of both indirect and direct forms, which highlight the effects of imperfect price-adjustment information which can result in price rigidity at non-market-clearing levels.

The possibility of disequilibrium unemployment creates the

potential for intervention by the central authorities to reduce the duration of any unemployment-creating disequilibrium (or, indeed, to actively generate positions of disequilibrium which are unemployment-reducing). The Keynesians have always advocated that unemployment can be reduced by macro policies designed to stimulate the level of aggregate demand. However, the theoretical rationale for such Keynesian policies has been severely undermined by the theoretical developments of the classical Keynesian school. By adopting a classical interpretation of Keynesian macro analysis, the classical Keynesians have shown, albeit possibly in a quite unintentional way, that the effectiveness of macro policies depends on the precise nature of the imperfections at the micro level which are ultimately causing unemployment. Recent classical Keynesians have tended to develop analyses of quantity constraints created by imperfect price-adjustment information. These quantity constraints are capable of being loosened by Keynesian demand-management policies. However, unemployment resulting from other types of imperfections may not be so amenable to Keynesian policies. For example, if the ultimate cause of unemployment is too high money wages as a result of structural imperfections in the form of the monopoly power of trade unions, Keynesian policies are only effective if they succeed in reducing the real wage by raising the aggregate price level relative to the money wage. However, if trade unions use their monopoly power to maintain the level of real wage, the effect of Keynesian policies is to generate a price–wage inflationary spiral with no positive effect on the level of employment. It was the recognition of this deficiency in Keynesian policies which led most Keynesians to advocate the need for incomes policies as a necessary complement to any expansion of aggregate demand.

The neoclassical/monetarist theory of the expectations-augmented Phillips curve suggested the possibility of using Keynesian policies to generate an unemployment-reducing position of disequilibrium. This requires that households underestimate the inflationary effects of expansionary policy, thereby overestimating the expected real wage. This leads households to offer a higher supply of labour than they would have done under conditions of correct expectations. Such unemployment-reducing policies can, at best, only be effective temporarily and, to the extent that agents adapt their expectations in the light of past experience, the central authorities would require to generate an accelerating inflation rate in order to maintain the higher level of employment. Such policies are not therefore a long-term solution. Indeed, the recent new classical critique disputes their effectiveness even in the short-term. If agents form their expectations rationally, there is no scope for the central authorities to engineer the appropriate mistakes in expectations through the use of any systematic policy. In the world of rational expectations, incorrect expectations only result from random factors such as exogenous shocks and policy 'surprises'.

A post-classical theory of involuntary unemployment

In *The General Theory*, Keynes claimed to have developed a theory of involuntary unemployment, a form of unemployment which classical theory could not deal with. Classical theory, Keynes argued, could only explain frictional and voluntary unemployment, not involuntary unemployment. The concept of involuntary unemployment required theoretical economists to move beyond the confines of the classical frame of reference. Most of the followers of Keynes, however, attempted to produce an orthodox synthesis between Keynes's macro analysis and classical micro analysis. This resulted in the development of the classical Keynesian reinterpretation of Keynes within the classical frame of reference. The inevitable result of the search for the classical microfoundations of Keynesian macroeconomics has been the elaboration of imperfectionist theories of macro misallocation. This has had the technological implication of casting doubt on the effectiveness of Keynesian demand-management policies as a means of reducing the level of unemployment in a capitalist economy.

It is the contention of the present analysis that Keynes's analysis of involuntary unemployment comes back into its own as a unique non-classical contribution if it is interpreted within the post-classical framework. This post-classical interpretation of involuntary unemployment requires that the processes which cause unemployment be analysed in terms of the actual behaviour patterns exhibited by firms and households. If this approach is adopted, the level of employment in a capitalist economy is no longer seen to be within the allocative mode of activity. The industrial sector does not operate as an exchange economy in which the level of employment is regulated by the price mechanism within markets. There is no aggregate market for labour in which employment and the real wage are determined simultaneously in an allocative process.

Rather than being an exchange economy, the industrial sector operates as a monetary production economy. The behaviour patterns exhibited by firms and households are such that the level of employment is determined within the utilization mode of activity. Involuntary unemployment results from the underutilization of industrial capital. Such a situation cannot arise in an exchange economy if the price mechanism is able to operate effectively. The allocative mode of activity involves, by definition, an automatic tendency towards the full utilization of industrial capital. Such an automatic self-adjustment process does not exist in a monetary production economy since there is no price mechanism at the aggregate level. The utilization mode of activity involves a non-allocative means of regulation, namely the multiplier process.

Involuntary unemployment in a monetary production economy is the macro consequence of the behaviour patterns of individual firms and households. The nature of the output and employment decisions of firms implies that the aggregate level of employment depends primarily on the level of aggregate demand. A monetary production economy is a demand side economy. The level of aggregate demand depends on the current rate of the monetary flow. Indeed, a monetary production economy is only in balance if the current rate of flow of money income equals the current rate of flow of money expenditure. This balance is brought about by the multiplier process in which the rate of the monetary flow itself adjusts to ensure that there is no net flow of funds between the industrial and financial sectors. The multiplier process results from the nature of the consumption decision of households as characterized by the Keynesian consumption function. The proportion of the flow of money income which households utilize as a flow of consumption expenditure depends on the rate of flow of money income. It follows that the rate of the monetary flow adjusts to ensure that investment equals savings, the equilibrium condition for the industrial sector. It was Keynes's abiding achievement to show that there is no reason to suppose that the rate of the investment flow adjusts to the level necessary to produce the rate of monetary flow required to maintain the full utilization of industrial capital and the full employment of labour.

Thus involuntary unemployment arises from any deficiency of aggregate demand consequent on the operation of the multiplier process, this causal process resulting from the behaviour patterns adopted by firms and households operating within the particular context of behaviour created by a monetary production economy. The involuntary nature of this type of unemployment has three interrelated dimensions. First, this unemployment is involuntary with respect to its causation. Involuntary unemployment is the unintended macro consequence of the behaviour patterns adopted by individual firms and households, given their context of behaviour. Involuntary unemployment is not the voluntary outcome of allocative choices by rational agents. Second, it follows that involuntary unemployment is involuntary with respect to its cure. A reduction in the level of involuntary unemployment requires an increase in the level of aggregate demand. But the level of aggregate demand is not under the control of any individual agent. To cure involuntary unemployment requires collective action by all agents. This leads on to the third dimension of involuntary unemployment. The involuntariness of this form of unemployment with respect to its causation and cure implies a moral responsibility on the part of the central authorities to take the necessary action. This is an ethical question involving judgements of value but one which cannot be separated from the analysis of the situation. All values are fact-laden, in the sense of being influenced by the particular circumstances in which they are issues, just as in the same way all facts are value-laden by virtue of their existence within a particular theoretical frame of reference.

The post-classical theory of involuntary unemployment has important technological implications. Indeed, it is these technological implications which are the main justification for the development of the post-classical theory. If the behavioural assumptions on which the post-classical analysis is founded are realistic, it follows that there is a rationale for the necessity of Keynesian demand-management policies on both technical and ethical grounds. Keynesian policies can raise the rate of inflow of funds into the monetary flow of the industrial sector. This generates a positive multiplier effect which results in an increase in the rate of the monetary flow. To the extent that Keynesian policies are successful in raising the rate of the monetary flow, this may have the result of increasing the aggregate level of utilization of industrial capital and the aggregate level of employment, thereby reducing the level of involuntary unemployment.

However, it cannot be stressed enough that the effectiveness of Keynesian policies is not a foregone conclusion. Keynesian policies can influence the rate of the monetary flow, but there is no one-to-one relationship between the rate of the monetary flow and the aggregate level of employment. The link across the Keynesian Dichotomy between the realm of the monetary flow and the realm of production is a tenuous one, subject to much fluctuation in its strength. Keynesian policies may be a necessary condition for the reduction of involuntary unemployment, but they are by no means a sufficient condition. Unfortunately, far too little attention in the past has been given by Keynesians to the possible insufficiency of Keynesian solutions. Too often, Keynesians have adopted a very mechanical approach to the operation of the capitalist economy in which the aggregate level of employment can simply be adjusted by pulling the particular levers available to the central authorities. Such an hydraulic view of the economic system seriously underestimates the problems of control which face the central authorities within a capitalist economy. The inevitable 'failures' which followed in the wake of this hydraulic view have been one of the main contributory factors in the current counter-revolution against Keynesian policy prescriptions.

The hydraulic approach to Keynesian policy prescriptions has tended to give too little emphasis to the importance of the state of confidence of those who managed the industrial capital stock. The state of confidence is one of the major determinants of the strength at any point in time of the link across the Keynesian Dichotomy between the realm of monetary flows and the realm of production. The state of confidence of those who manage the industrial capital stock affects all of their decisions, including those on output and employment levels. Yet Keynesians have tended to take a very restrictive view of the effects of the state of confidence. Partly this is a result of Keynes himself, who tended to limit his discussion of the state of confidence in the industrial sector to its effects on the state of long-term expectations on which the investment decision is based. However, the state of confidence also tends to affect the short-term expectations associated with the output and employment decisions. Thus the state of confidence determines whether a decline in the absolute rate (or the rate of acceleration) of the current monetary flow has a relatively minor effect on the level of activity in the industrial sector or whether it sets off a cumulative process of contraction in the level of activity. Likewise, the state of confidence determines whether an increase in the rate of the current monetary flow engineered through Keynesian demand-management policies has little effect on the level of activity or sets off a cumulative process of expansion.

The state of confidence, as Keynes so eloquently pointed out, is a matter of belief, not calculation. It is based on instinct, feelings and the customary, but logically unfounded, acceptance of the principle of continuity that the future will resemble the past. This principle of continuity underlies every inductive proposition which is arrived at logically, but is itself incapable of logical proof. The state of confidence depends on the nature of the underlying systems of belief and expectation which provide the necessary basis for human decision-making involving the future. The logical calculations which make up the decision-making process tend to blind the theorist of human behaviour to their tacit, non-logical foundations.

The state of confidence tends to exhibit a self-reinforcing nature. Once arrived at, by whatever means, the state of confidence acts as a frame of reference which tends to exert a tacit influence on the perceptions of human decision-makers. We tend to see what our beliefs allow us to see. This bounded vision serves to reinforce the degree of belief which human decision-makers have in their existing perceptions of the world, unless a sufficiently significant observation or series of similar observations leads to the abandonment of the existing system of beliefs. Inasmuch as human agents are interdependent, there is a tendency for a conventional system of beliefs to emerge which is shared by the majority. This conventional view determines the state of confidence in the economy at any point in time. The state of confidence also operates in a self-reinforcing manner by generating specific expectations which, in turn, induce specific actions which bring about the actualization of the previously expected results. This occurs in the financial sector in the form of speculative activity. The industrial sector can also exhibit the phenomenon of self-fulfilling prophecy. If firms do not expect any permanent increase in the level of aggregate demand for their products, these expectations can result in a reluctance to expand output and employment in response to any rise in aggregate demand, and thereby bring about its expected reversal.

The self-reinforcing nature of the state of confidence, at both the level of perception and the level of action, can lead the economy to become locked into what could be called a 'field of expectations'. This field could be one of constancy in which firms and households expect the level of activity to remain relatively unchanged and, in acting accordingly, bring about the actualization of the expected constancy. Two types of field of constancy are possible. First, there is an expansionary field in which the economy operates at a relatively high level of activity. In contrast, the economy may become locked into a recessionary field in which the level of activity is relatively low. An alternative form of field of expectations is one of change in which firms and households expect a significant change in the level of activity in the economy and act accordingly, thus bringing about the expected sharp change. The field of change can act in either an upward or a downward direction.

It seems likely that the normal state of affairs is for a capitalist economy to settle within a field of constancy, of either an expansionary or recessionary type. Partly this is the result of the bootstraps effect of the predominant tendency in human belief to expect that stability is the normal state of affairs. It is also the result of the tendency of periods of significant change to be brought to a halt by the emergence of constraints to further change. For example, the full utilization of industrial capital and the full employment of labour act as twin ceilings on any upward movement in the level of activity in the short run. It follows, therefore, that through historical time a capitalist economy is likely to exhibit relatively long periods of dynamic stability in the level of activity when the economy is in a field of constancy, punctuated by occasional, relatively short periods of significant movements in the level of activity when the economy enters a field of change. Thus the capitalist economy is likely to move in a process of punctuated equilibrium.

These fields of expectations can exist at different, interdependent levels. For example, although an economy may be in a field of constancy with a stable level of activity, there may still be short-term, cyclical variations in the level of activity around the longer-term norm.

The recognition of the importance of the state of confidence is a necessary requirement in the overall assessment of the likely effects of Keynesian policies on the level of involuntary unemployment. If a capitalist economy is locked into a recessionary field of expectations, the central authorities are likely to have only a very limited scope for influencing the level of employment. Any really significant reduction in the level of involuntary unemployment in such circumstances requires, as a necessary condition, that the economy breaks out of its existing field of expectations. It is unlikely that the central authorities on their own possess the power to engineer such a revolutionary change in the field of expectations, yet, without such a change, Keynesian policies are doomed to relative impotence. In such circumstances, the only realistic arm's-length option open to the central authorities may be the one of ensuring no adverse movements in the current monetary flow while waiting to 'ride the wave' created by any sufficiently large positive exogenous shock to the economic system. Such a policy conclusion is very restricted, particularly with respect to the grandiose claims of the old Keynesians, but it may be the best arm's-length policy there really is and must be accepted as such, however disappointing. Yet it should not be forgotten that even the acceptance of these much-restricted Keynesian policy prescriptions would, in the current climate of economic opinion, constitute a considerable step forward in reclaiming the ground lost to the advocates of the traditional classical policy of *laissez-faire* who deny entirely any possibility of effective macroeconomic intervention by the central authorities.

Inflation

Classical theory has tended to focus on one particular type of inflation, namely macro-pull inflation. Macro-pull inflation occurs when the rate of the monetary flow in the industrial sector increases relative to the rate of flow of aggregate output. The possibility of such a situation is created by the Keynesian Dichotomy. There is no reason why the rate of the monetary flow should exhibit a one-to-one relationship with the level of activity in the realm of production, even although they are inextricably linked through the aggregate demand mechanism. As has been argued at several points in the present analysis, there are a number of reasons why the strength of the aggregate demand mechanism may vary, the most important of these being the state of confidence and the associated expectations which hold sway in the minds of the managers of the industrial capital stock at any point in time. Thus it is possible that industrial firms may not react to any potential change in the rate of the monetary flow by an immediate equiproportionate increase in the rate of the output flow.

If circumstances emerge in which the rate of the monetary flow has the potential to increase relative to the rate of flow of aggregate output, this creates a potential gap which must be bridged. One possible way is by an increase in the aggregate price level. In this case the gap takes the form of an inflationary gap in which the aggregate price level plays the allocative role of ensuring that there is market-clearing in the aggregate goods market with equality between the monetary value of aggregate demand and the monetary value of aggregate supply. It does not necessarily follow, however, that any potential excess in the monetary flow over the output flow should become an inflationary gap. It is possible that industrial firms might react to any potential gap by attempting to reschedule the monetary and production flows over time. Thus any potential increase in aggregate demand could lead to the lengthening of the duration of any period of waiting by consumers for delivery of purchased goods and services. In this way industrial firms use the timing of production as the allocative mechanism with which to balance the monetary and production flows. This temporal means of allocative regulation has the effect of preventing the potential gap from ever being actualized.

In its analysis of macro-pull inflation, classical theory has tended to concentrate on one particular form of macro-pull inflation, the so-called demand-pull inflation. Demand-pull inflation occurs when the rate of growth in the monetary value of aggregate demand cannot be matched by an equal rate of growth in the aggregate supply of output because of the full utilization of the existing industrial capital stock and the full employment of labour. Full employment acts as the ultimate constraint on any expansion of productive activity in a capitalist economy. If the monetary value of aggregate demand continues to grow after the economy has reached the full-employment ceiling, the result is the appearance of an inflationary gap with the aggregate price level acting as the allocative mechanism to ensure market-clearing in the aggregate goods market. Within classical theory, the main division of opinion with regard to demand-pull inflation is over the ultimate cause of the excess demand. Theorists of a Keynesian persuasion have located the cause as an excessive level of autonomous expenditures, such as investment, which imply, through the multiplier process, an equilibrium level of money income which is greater than the full-employment level of output valued at the current aggregate price level. In recent years this Keynesian analysis has been disputed by the monetarist school of thought. The monetarists hold a modern form of the quantity theory of money so that the ultimate cause of any demand-pull inflation is seen to be an exogenously determined increase in the supply of money.

The post-classical analysis of inflation recognizes the possibility of demand-pull inflation, in which the aggregate price level plays an allocative role within the aggregate goods market. The allocative function is one role for price, as explained by classical theory. The important point is that the allocative role is not the only role for price, despite the assertions of classical theorists to the contrary. In accepting the classical analysis the demand-pull inflation, this does mean coming down on the side of the Keynesians in their dispute with the monetarists, since the Keynesian macro analysis is based on the multiplier process, the means of regulation in a monetary production economy. The monetarist analysis, however, runs directly counter to the theory of a monetary production economy over the issue of the determination of the supply of money. In the modern capitalist economy, the supply of money is primarily endogenously determined, in complete opposition to the mythical beliefs of the monetarists.

The post-classical theory of inflation seeks to generalize the classical theory of demand-pull inflation in two ways. First, it should be recognized that demand-pull inflation is only one particular form of the more general phenomenon of macro-pull inflation. Macro-pull inflation occurs whenever there is the potential for the monetary flow to increase relative to the output flow. The output flow may be constrained for reasons other than the full-employment constraint. An inflationary gap could arise if the output flow is constrained by virtue of pessimistic expectations on the part of the managers of the industrial capital stock. Indeed, there is even no necessity for macro-pull inflation to be associated with a stagnant or slowly increasing output flow. It is possible that an inflationary gap could emerge because the output flow has declined in absolute terms, possibly as the result of the economy moving into an expectational field of downward change.

The post-classical theory of inflation also seeks to generalize beyond the classical theory of inflation by incorporating a second type of inflation which results from a very different causal process to that of the allocative-induced macro-pull inflation. The second type of inflation which is possible in a monetary production economy is micro-push inflation. This type of inflation results from the non-allocative roles performed by prices and wages. It is the type of inflation which has been explained by the non-classical theories of cost-push inflation.

The possibility of micro-push inflation is created by the interaction between the various non-allocative functions of prices and wages. Together these non-allocative functions can lead to a wage-price inflationary spiral with its own internal self-sustaining dynamic. The key non-allocative mechanism which can create this inflationary spiral is the conductive role of prices and wages. Price plays a conductive role for industrial firms by passing on any increase in unit costs of production in the form of higher prices to the consumers, thereby protecting their profit margins. This conductive role of price occurs through the adoption of mark-up pricing rules. The money wage also plays a conductive role inasmuch as workers bargain for a real-wage objective. If the aggregate price level rises, workers will attempt to maintain the purchasing power of their money wages by bargaining for an increase in money wages which is equiproportionate to the increase in the aggregate price level.

The conductive role of prices and wages creates a self-reinforcing transmission mechanism for a rise in the aggregate price level. A rise in the general level of money wages produces a rise in the aggregate price level through the mark-up pricing of industrial firms, while any rise in the aggregate price level will provoke a rise in the general level of money wages through the real-wage bargaining objectives of workers. All that is required is a trigger to set this potential in motion. One obvious source of such a trigger is an imbalance at the macro level between the monetary flow and the production flow. This is the situation of macro-pull inflation, where the non-allocative transmission mechanisms at the micro level act as the means of realizing the necessary allocative adjustment in prices and wages. However, although the need for an allocative adjustment may provide the initial trigger, the self-sustaining nature of the conductive role of prices and wages means that the inflationary process can continue beyond that necessary for the allocative adjustment. At this point the non-allocative behaviour patterns take over in their own right. They are no longer the passive means of transmission for allocative pressures, but become the active creators of a non-allocative inflation.

A non-allocative inflation need not have its origins in the need for an allocative adjustment at the macro level. The trigger for a wage–price spiral may itself be non-allocative in nature. This may take the form of an exogenous shock to the economy. Alternatively, a non-allocative inflation may be triggered by the operation of the other non-allocative roles of price and wages beyond the purely conductive role. Prices and wages fulfil a strategic function in the competitive interaction between firms and between groups of workers, respectively. Thus, for example, a rise in the money wage of one group of workers, for whatever reason, may set in motion the latent dynamic within the wage-bargaining process created by the concern of workers for the relative level of their wages with respect to other groups of workers. Hence a rise in the money wage of one or more groups of workers, who are regarded as in some way as 'leaders' in the round of wage bargains, may produce a general rise in money wages, with all the consequent possibilities of a generalized inflationary spiral which this would entail. Again, the underlying trigger may be a macro allocative one, but this is by no means a necessity. There are a multitude of non-allocative reasons which could lead a group of workers to bargain for relative higher money wages. A micro-push inflation could also be set in motion by the financial role of price. If there is a generalized desire on the part of industrial firms to generate additional profits for financial reasons, this may result in an increase in the aggregate price level, resulting in an inflationary spiral. Such a generalized financial stimulus could be created by the need for industrial firms to generate internal funds to finance a general boom in investment, consequent on a sufficiently marked improvement in the field of expectations.

The interaction of the conductive role of prices and wages, coupled with the potential for non-allocative triggers of sufficient magnitude, creates the possibility of a micro-push inflation of a very different nature to that of a macro-pull inflation, with, as a consequence, very different technological implications with regards to prescriptions for the appropriate anti-inflationary policies. The whole structure of industrial prices and money wages can take on the same bootstraps property possessed by financial prices and interest rates. Prices and wages in the industrial sector can generate their own internal dynamic, both separately and interactively. The whole structure of prices and wages can move in an upwards direction in a self-sustaining cumulative process of causation quite independently of any macro allocative pressure generated by an imbalance between the monetary flow and the output flow. With the honourable exception of the cost-push theorists, the overwhelming preoccupation of most theoretical economists with the allocative mode of activity has led them to largely ignore the self-perpetuating nature of the inflationary process, preferring instead the demand-pull theories, with their ability to give the inflationary process the firm reductionist foundation so desired by those who remain within the classical schools of thought. It is yet another example of the power of orthodoxy to have a highly restrictive special theory accepted as the only generally true theory.

The internal dynamic of prices and wages tends to be asymmetric in nature. Although prices and wages tend to move freely in an upward direction, they tend to be rigid downwards. This creates a ratchet effect over time where any cyclical pattern in the ultimate causes of inflation does not result in a cyclical pattern in the direction of movement of the aggregate price level. This asymmetry in the movement of prices and wages is mainly the result of their strategic role. Industrial firms, which are confronted by intense oligopolistic competitive pressure, are unlikely to be willing to pass on lower production costs in the form of lower prices for fear of instigating a price war with their competitors. Likewise, individual groups of workers are unlikely to be prepared to accept any cut in their money wages, despite the potential for a fall in the aggregate price level, since if the cut in money wages is not generalized in an equiproportional manner across all groups of workers, it implies a fall in the relative wage levels of those who accept the cut relative to those who are unwilling to risk any loss of comparability and able to resist the imposition of any such cuts. Such behaviour on the part of workers is entirely reasonable in the absence of a single centralized wage-bargaining process, as well as with respect to industrial firms themselves being unable, in the presence of oligopolistic pressures, to actualize any potential for the reduction of the aggregate price level without some centrally imposed dictum to do so.

Finally, any post-classical theory of inflation would be incomplete without an analysis of the likely effects of the positional role of prices and wages. Within the capitalist economy, there is an endemic conflict between the interests of industrial firms and the interests of households. This is the result of the structure of the capitalist economy being characterized by the pursuit of self-interest by individual firms and households through the exchange relationship. In this exchange relationship, industrial firms seek to generate a flow of profits, the rate of the profit flow depending on the rate of the output flow and the profit margin per unit of production. Ultimately the unit profit margin is a reflection of the difference between price and unit wage costs. Industrial firms seek to maximize this difference. Households, on the other hand, inasmuch as they depend on wages for income, wish to minimize the profit margin, in effect, since wages represent their unit of revenue while price represents their unit of expenditure. The outcome of this conflict at any point in time depends on the positions of relative power held by industrial capital in general. These positions of relative power take two forms. First, there is the power of firms *vis-à-vis* households with respect to the aggregate price level, reflecting the positions of relative power in the exchange of produced output. The second form of positional power occurs in the wage bargain between employers and employees, reflecting the positions of relative power in the exchange of labour services. Any change in either or both of these positions of relative power, or in the propensity with which agents actualize the potential gains from positional power, can trigger an inflationary spiral. The positional inflation which results from changes in positional power, or the propensity with which it is used, may go hand-in-hand with macro-pull inflation to the extent that positional power depends, at least in part, on the allocative process. For example, conditions of full employment may lead to workers demanding higher wages as a result of the positional power conferred by the scarcity of labour. The inflation which results under such circumstances should not be considered as merely demand-pull inflation. Demand-pull inflation requires not only conditions of full employment but also the presence of excess

not

aggregate demand. Positional inflation does need the presence of any excess demand. Furthermore, positional inflation does not even require the existence of full employment. It can occur whenever there is a change in positional power, or the propensity with which it is used, for whatever reason, economic or non-economic.

The unemployment–inflation relationship: a post-classical view of the Phillips curve debate

The Keynesian demand-pull theory of inflation implied that there would be a unique relationship between the unemployment rate and the rate of price inflation. This relationship resulted from the Keynesian belief that unemployment and inflation are the two sides of the same coin. Unemployment occurs in periods of deficient aggregate demand, while inflation occurs in periods of excess aggregate demand. This Keynesian view of the unemployment–inflation relationship is enshrined in the original Phillips curve, the observation of a stable inverse statistical association between the rate of unemployment and the rate of wage inflation. The discovery of the Phillips curve in the late 1950s seemed to provide the empirical confirmation of the Keynesian demand-pull theory of inflation.

The historical experience of capitalist economies from the mid-1960s onwards, however, began to provide the opposite verdict on the Keynesian demand-pull theory. Capitalist economies have been subject to a period of stagflation, the simultaneous occurrence of high rates of unemployment with high rates of inflation. Such a phenomenon is in direct conflict with the Keynesian demand-pull theory. Capitalist economies have exhibited high rates of inflation at times when they are clearly operating far below their full-employment ceilings. The Phillips curve had broken down, and with its demise Keynesian economics entered a period of crisis in the theoretical circles of the academic community as well as in the domain of public policy prescription.

The crisis in Keynesian economics created the fertile ground needed for the classical counter-revolution led by the monetarist school. The Keynesian demand-pull theory foundered on its adoption of a single causal explanation for both unemployment and inflation. The monetarist view of the unemployment–inflation relationship did not suffer from any such hostage to fortune. According to the monetarist explanation, unemployment results from the misallocation on the supply side of the economy caused by wage rigidities in the labour market, whereas inflation results from the allocative process of regulation on the demand side necessitated by excessive growth in the money supply. In equilibrium the economy would come to rest at the natural rate of unemployment, with a rate of price inflation equal to the rate of growth of the money supply. This analysis is itself enshrined in the expectations-augmented Phillips curve, the monetarist reformulation of the original Phillips curve. The monetarist theory of the unemployment–inflation relationship represents an advance within classical theory over the Keynesian demand-pull approach since it can explain the phenomenon of stagflation. The monetarist theory also provided some recognition of the importance of inflationary expectations, albeit only in the context of the disequilibrium adjustments within the allocative process.

Despite the almost universal acceptance of the expectations-augmented Phillips curve within economic theory, this present analysis rejects the monetarist view as appropriate for the understanding of the modern capitalist economy. The monetarist view is based on two classical doctrines which are entirely misleading as representations of the actual behaviour patterns to be found in the industrial sector. First, the notion of the natural rate of unemployment is based on the belief that there is an aggregate market for labour. The post-classical view is that no such market exists. Second, the monetarist view remains wedded to the belief that the supply of money is exogenously determined. Again, this belief runs entirely counter to the post-classical theory of money provided by the present analysis.

The post-classical view of the unemployment–inflation relationship begins with the belief that the level of unemployment is determined within the utilization mode of activity, the key influence being the rate of the monetary flow as regulated by the multiplier process. The rate of inflation, on the other hand, can be determined either by a wholly allocative process, as in the case of macro-pull inflation, or, alternatively, by a variety of non-allocative processes, as in the case of micro-push inflation. Demand-pull is one, and only one, type of inflation. The mistake on the part of some Keynesian theorists was to suppose demand-pull inflation to be the only type of inflation. The phenomenon of stagflation showed the limitations of this particular view, but at the cost of the almost near-extinction of the whole Keynesian enterprise, in both its classical and non-classical forms, as a recognizable approach to economic theory and policy. Once the Keynesian approach is placed within the firmer foundations provided by the post-classical approach, stagflation is no longer a theoretical problem casting doubt on the essential truths of a monetary production economy. Thus the Keynesian myth of a stable Phillips curve can be laid to rest alongside the monetarist myths of the exogenously determined money supply and the aggregate labour market which, paradoxically, it helped to revive. The Keynesians have been as prone to creating such myths as all other theoretical economists have been from time to time.

Towards a post-classical theory of macroeconomic policy

The capitalist dilemma

The Phillips curve analysis, in both its original Keynesian and its later monetarist forms, presents policy-makers with a trade-off at the macro level between the rate of unemployment and the rate of price inflation. In particular, lower unemployment can be gained only at the expense of higher inflation. In its original Keynesian form, this unemployment–inflation trade-off was seen as a long-term trade-off between different positions of equilibrium. This view no longer holds. The current orthodoxy, based on the expectations-augmented Phillips curve of monetarist analysis, denies that there is any long-term equilibrium trade-off between unemployment and inflation. In equilibrium the supply side of the economy moves to the natural rate of unemployment while the demand side generates a rate of price inflation equal to the rate of growth of the money supply. Any unemployment–inflation trade-off can only occur over the short-term period of disequilibrium adjustment, provided that agents operate with the appropriate incorrect expectations of the inflationary effects of the macroeconomic policies adopted by the central authorities. However, as the recent new classical critique has shown, even the restricted short-term view of the unemployment–inflation trade-off presented by the monetarist school is itself an overstatement of the likely effectiveness of macroeconomic policy. If agents form their expectations in accordance with the rational-expectations hypothesis, the use of macroeconomic policy in any systematic manner is entirely impotent with regard to engineering any change in the rate of unemployment away from the natural rate. In such circumstances, only policy 'surprises' which are unexpected by agents can have any effect, even in the short-term.

The notion that there is an unemployment–inflation trade-off is a reflection of the tendency of orthodox theorists to take a unitary view of the capitalist economy. Unemployment and inflation are treated as problems for the economy as a whole. Policy-makers are faced with a choice over which particular outcome is socially optimal. This is not the case. Within the capitalist economy, unemployment and inflation represent problems for different sectors of the economy. Unemployment is primarily a problem for the industrial sector, while inflation is primarily a problem for the financial sector. The unitary view of the economy adopted by classical theorists obscures the fact that the unemployment–inflation trade-off is a trade-off between the interests of the industrial sector and the interests of the financial sector. Such a conflict never exists in the classical view of the world, where the doctrine of the invisible hand teaches that the price mechanism is able to render the individual pursuit of self-interest consistent with the general welfare of all. The doctrine of the invisible hand is the most sacred of all classical beliefs. It is the central message of the post-classical approach that the dualistic nature of the capitalist economy means that the doctrine of the invisible hand is but a myth, albeit one with an incredible hold over the minds of theoretical and practical economists. Once economists have freed themselves from the myth of the invisible hand, they can begin to come to terms with the conflicts of interest which exist within the capitalist economy. It may not be the world which economists desire, but it is the world which exists in the here-and-now and the one of which it is the moral responsibility of economists to gain an understanding.

The existence of involuntary unemployment represents a problem for the industrial sector. Involuntary unemployment means the underutilization of resources within the industrial sector. This restricts the employment opportunities available to households, thereby preventing some households from having direct access to the monetary flow as a source of income, with the poverty and hardship which this entails for those who depend on wage income to provide their means of subsistence. Involuntary unemployment also runs counter to the interests of industrial capital since it implies the underutilization of the industrial capital stock with the consequence that the profits flow is restricted.

Involuntary unemployment is not a fundamental problem as such for the financial sector. Agents in the financial sector gain a return from the ownership of financial capital which is, by its very nature, always fully utilized. Involuntary unemployment in the industrial sector has only a secondary impact on the financial sector. To the extent that involuntary unemployment is associated with the rate of the monetary flow being less than its potential rate of flow, given the existing aggregate price level, it follows that the rate of flow of funds between the industrial and financial sectors is less than the potential rate of flow, with the consequence that the financial institutions face restrictions in the supply of new profitable opportunities to engage in transfers of purchasing power. The relatively lower rate of profit flow in the industrial sector may lead to a fall in the market values of equity capital, and the spillover effects consequent on this, to the extent that lower profits lead to lower dividend payments and, hence a fall in the overall net rate of return from equity capital relative to other forms of assets. Finally, the existence of involuntary unemployment may affect the financial sector through the expectations which it gives rise to on the part of financial agents. In particular, financial agents may expect the central authorities to adopt more expansionary macroeconomic policies, leading to an increase in the supply of debt in the case of a fiscal expansion, or a fall in the base rate of interest in the case of a monetary expansion. Financial agents will expect that these expansionary policies will cause changes in the market values of traded assets. These expectations may spark off a wave of speculative activity, resulting in the actualization of the expected changes in the market values of traded assets.

Inflation is primarily a problem for the financial sector. From the point of view of financial agents, the aggregate price level represents the terms of exchange between financial wealth and currently produced goods and services. The occurrence of inflation means that the aggregate price level is increasing, implying an adverse movement in the terms of exchange for financial agents. Inflation reduces the real value of the accumulated stock of financial wealth. There is no automatic mechanism to ensure that the overall net rate of return from financial assets rises in order to offset the decline in the real value of the stock of financial wealth. Indeed, the allocative process set in motion by the occurrence of inflation may lead to a reduction in the nominal value of financial capital to the extent that the overall net rate of return moves upwards through a fall in the market value of traded assets.

Inflation is much less of a problem for the industrial sector because of the conductive role of prices and wages. Industrial firms use mark-up pricing to protect the real value of the profits flow while employed workers bargain for a real-wage objective. The conductive role of prices and wages gives automatic inflation-proofing for those with direct access to the monetary flow, provided they have sufficient power to ensure that the conductive function is fully operative. Obviously inflation remains a problem for those with no direct access to the monetary flow or with insufficient power to ensure an adequate conductive adjustment in prices and wages. Some inflation may be beneficial for the industrial sector inasmuch as it helps promote a higher level of activity. This can occur through a reduction in the real value of the fixed interest and debt repayments of those industrial firms and households who have financed previous expenditures by means of debt. To the extent that debtors are likely to have a higher propensity to spend relative to asset holders, the increase in aggregate demand from the improvement in the position of debtors as the result of inflation is likely to more than offset any fall in aggregate demand from the negative wealth effect on asset holders as the real value of their assets falls. Thus, overall, some inflation is likely to produce a net stimulus to aggregate demand and, in turn, to output and employment levels.

The recognition of the differential impact of unemployment and inflation on the industrial and financial sectors creates the possibility of a dilemma for policy-makers. It may be the case that macroeconomic policies cannot be used to pursue an objective in the interests of one sector without a detrimental impact on the other sector. If this trade-off in policy objectives exists, policy-makers face the dilemma of having to make a decision over the priority of the employment and inflation objectives. Such a decision represents a decision between the interests of the industrial and financial sectors. A reduction in the level of involuntary unemployment is a priority for those who are unemployed as well as for industrial firms, who can reap a higher rate of profit flow if there is a higher level of utilization of the industrial capital stock. The reduction in the rate of inflation is a priority for those with financial wealth. Thus, to the extent that policy-makers in a capitalist economy must face a choice between employment and inflation objectives, they can be said to face the capitalist dilemma of having to decide between the interests of industrial capital and the interests of financial capital.

The experience of Keynesian and monetarist policy regimes has shown the extent of the capitalist dilemma. The Keynesian policy regime can be seen as giving priority to the industrial sector by using fiscal and monetary policies to increase the rate of the monetary flow in order to achieve a full-employment level of productive activity. The monetarist policy regime, on the other hand, clearly gives priority to the interests of financial sector over the industrial sector. In effect, monetarist policies attempt to lower the rate of inflation by restricting the rate of monetary flow, with the inevitable consequences of higher levels of involuntary unemployment and the associated reduction in the rate of utilization of the industrial capital stock.

Keynesian demand-management reconsidered

Keynesian demand-management offers the central authorities an arm's-length means of raising the aggregate level of employment. Keynesian policies seek to reach their employment objective by increasing the level of aggregate demand in the economy. This is achieved by inducing a multiplier expansion of the rate of the monetary flow through the creation of an additional net inflow of funds into the industrial sector. The central authorities can use either fiscal policy or monetary policy or some combination of the two to generate the necessary net inflow of funds into the industrial sector.

Fiscal policy offers a direct means of controlling the net inflow of funds into the industrial sector using the instruments of government expenditure and taxation. Government expenditure represents an injection of funds into the current monetary flow while taxation represents a leakage. Both are under the direct control of the central authorities. An additional net inflow of funds into the industrial sector occurs whenever the central authorities increase the budget deficit, the excess of government expenditure over taxation. This budget deficit is financed by means of the issue of government debt, a form of traded asset. It is possible for the central authorities to generate a net injection of funds into the monetary process through an equal increase in the level of government expenditure and taxation which leaves the budget deficit unchanged. This is known as the balanced budget multiplier effect. It results from the fact that part of the increase in taxation is funded by a reduction in savings and, therefore, does not represent an additional leakage of funds from the monetary flow. The balanced budget multiplier effect can only produce a relatively limited stimulus. Any significant fiscal stimulus to the monetary flow requires an increase in the budget deficit.

An alternative method by which the central authorities can attempt to control the rate of the monetary flow is through the indirect means of monetary policy. Monetary policy involves the adoption of a managed regime by the central bank for the determination of the base rate of interest. By reducing the base rate of interest, the central authorities can engineer a reduction in the whole structure of bank interest rates with the intention of producing a positive effect on the net flow of funds from the financial sector to the industrial sector. In particular, the reduction in interest rates could stimulate the rate of the investment expenditure flow. Thus monetary policy is an indirect mechanism since it aims to increase the rate of the monetary flow in the industrial sector as a spillover effect of actions aimed at the financial sector. The effectiveness of monetary policy depends crucially on the sensitivity of the flows between the industrial and financial sectors to changes in interest rates. Keynesian behavioural assumptions suggest that it is likely that these flows are relatively insensitive to changes in interest rates. The outflow of savings to the industrial sector is primarily determined by the rate of the current monetary flow, while the inflow of investment is determined by the state of long-term expectations and, through the accelerator mechanism, by recent changes in the rate of the monetary flow. It is for this reason that many Keynesians have adopted a fiscalist stance, advocating the use of fiscal policy rather than monetary policy as the means with which to control the rate of the monetary flow.

The choice between the use of fiscal and monetary policies for demand-management reflects the extent of the capitalist dilemma which faces policy-makers. Fiscal policy offers the most effective means of controlling the rate of the monetary flow since it operates directly on the flow of funds between the industrial and financial sectors. However, the issue of new government debt on the stock market which is implied by an increase in the budget deficit is likely to depress market prices of the existing stock of traded assets, to the detriment of those who are currently holding their wealth in this form. Thus the benefits of a fiscal expansion for the unemployed and industrial capital are achieved at the expense of financial agents. Monetary policy, on the other hand, implies a very different distribution of benefits and costs. Since it is an indirect means of controlling the rate of the monetary flow, dependent on the inter-sectoral flow of funds being sufficiently sensitive to changes in interest rates, monetary policy offers a relatively ineffective method of influencing the industrial sector in contrast to the more direct method of fiscal expansion. But while being less desirable from the standpoint of the unemployed and industrial sector, it is more desirable for the holders of financial wealth to the extent that any fall in the base rate of interest stimulates a general rise in the market values of traded assets.

The effectiveness of fiscal policy in raising the rate of the monetary flow is reduced to the extent that an increase in the budget deficit generates a negative-feedback effect on the monetary flow through the impact of the issue of new government debt on the behavior of the financial sector. The issue of new government debt is likely to depress the current market values of traded assets, which may have the knock-on effect of reducing the net flow of funds to the industrial sector. This negative-feedback effect of a fiscal expansion is known as the crowding-out effect. It can occur in a two main ways. First, the fall in the market value of part of the accumulated stock of financial wealth may have a direct negative wealth effect on the rate of expenditure flows by households and firms in the industrial sector. Second, the fall in the market prices of traded assets may lead to an upward movement in the whole structure of bank interest rates if the central bank operates a market regime for the determination of the base rate of interest. Any general rise in interest rates may tend to reduce the net flow of funds to the industrial sector. Following the Keynesian behaviour assumptions, it is likely that both these mechanisms of the crowding-out effect are relatively insignificant. In any case, the crowding-out effect can be offset by combining an expansionary fiscal policy with an expansionary monetary policy.

Keynesian demand-management, in both its fiscal and monetary forms, suffers from the major weakness that it is an arm's-length attempt to raise the level of productive activity in the industrial sector. Keynesian policies can only effect the rate of the monetary flow and hence fall foul of the uncertainties created by the Keynesian Dichotomy. The link between the realm of the monetary flow and the realm of productive activity is a very tenuous one subject to much fluctuation in its strength. In particular, the propensity of industrial capital to increase its rate of utilization in response to an increase in the rate of the current monetary flow is very dependent on the nature of the expectational field in which the economy is located. Insufficient confidence in the minds of the managers of the industrial capital stock can render Keynesian demand-management utterly ineffective as a means of raising the aggregate level of employment. In this respect, fiscal policy offers an important advantage over monetary policy. Government expenditure can be directed towards those industries which have the highest employment propensities. The central authorities can go further, using government expenditure to finance direct intervention in the realm of productive activity and taking over control of employment decisions either by setting up new productive activities under its own control or by assuming control of existing productive activities. Such direct intervention may become a necessity in times of deep recession. If arm's-length Keynesian demand-management is used in an attempt to create employment in times when the output and employment propensities are very low, the result may be a macro-pull inflation which can develop into an inflationary spiral with its own internal dynamic.

Anti-inflationary policies

Classical theory suggests that the objective of lower inflation be achieved by reducing the level of aggregate demand. This follows from the belief that inflation is demand-pull in nature. In the Keynesian version of this analysis, the source of excess aggregate demand is too high a level of autonomously-determined net injections into the aggregate flow of expenditures. In the monetarist version, the ultimate cause of excess aggregate demand is excessive growth in the money supply. This demand-pull analysis, in both its Keynesian and monetarist versions, points towards the need for reductions in the rate of the monetary flow or its rate of acceleration. This is achieved by restrictive fiscal and/or monetary policies. The main difference between Keynesian and monetarist versions of the demand-pull theory lies in the explanation of the transmission mechanisms involved rather than in the policies prescribed. However, to the extent that Keynesians adopt a fiscalist stance, they tend to advocate the use of fiscal policy, whereas monetarists are usually associated with the advocacy of monetary policy, since control of the money supply is the ultimate cure for inflation. Yet monetarists also tend to favour restrictive fiscal policies, seeing budget deficits as the cause of excessive growth in the money supply.

The Keynesian–monetarist consensus over anti-inflationary policies breaks down when it comes to prescriptions for stag-flationary situations. The Keynesian demand-pull theory cannot explain stagflation and gives contradictory policy prescriptions – stimulate aggregate demand to lower unemployment, but restrict aggregate demand to lower inflation. Both policies cannot oper-ate simultaneously. The usual Keynesian response has been to either ignore the inflationary aspects of the situation or to make some plea for the imposition of some form of incomes policy. The monetarists face no such problems with their analysis. Unemploy-ment is the result of problems on the supply side and needs to be dealt with by the appropriate supply-side policies. Inflation, accord-ing to the monetarists, is always caused by excessive growth in the money supply. Thus the only appropriate anti-inflationary policy is the demand-side policy of restricting the monetary flow.

The consequences of the monetarist approach are a matter of historical record for all to see, except the most committed propo-nents of this dangerous myth. Restricting the rate of the monet-ary flow is a very effective means of inducing a downturn in the rate of the output flow, with all the consequences of mass un-employment and underutilization of industrial capital which this entails. Stagflation is not an example of demand-pull inflation, and to treat it as such serves only to make matters worse. The experience of capitalist economies under a monetarist regime is the most extreme example of what happens when a faith founded on false beliefs is taken to its own logical conclusions. The poverty and deprivation of all those who have suffered as a result of monetarist policies should be on the conscience of all econ-omists who have propounded these absurd, misleading and dangerous doctrines. Theoretical economists have a moral responsibilty towards the victims of their false myths.

Anti-inflationary policies which involve restricting the monetary flow are only appropriate in circumstances of demand-pull inflation. Under such conditions, these policies should have no adverse effect on the level of productive activity, if judiciously applied. Other forms of macro-pull inflation do not need intervention of the demand-side. In these cases, the inflationary problem stems from a failure of the productive flow to respond to the monetary flow. It is this failure on the supply-side to which policy efforts need to be directed. Although restricting the monetary flow may appear, on the face of things, to be one means of solving the allocative imbalance between aggregate demand and supply, there is every possibility that industrial firms may respond by reducing the output flow rather than by reducing their propensity to increase prices.

Micro-push inflation needs to be controlled by the imposition of temporary limitations on the rate of increase of prices and wages. These limitations can halt the internal dynamic of the wage–price inflationary spiral created by the interaction of the conductive role of prices and wages. Such temporary limitations, in the form of a prices and incomes policy, are only successful if they prevent the internal dynamic of the inflationary policy from being set in motion without interfering in the normal adjustment process which must always follow in the wake of whatever shock to the economy which has triggered the inflationary process. Prices and incomes policies must allow industrial firms to adjust their prices in order to maintain profitability in the face of the inflationary shock, while workers must be able to achieve their real and relative wage objectives in the wage bargain. Intervention needs to take place after these normal adjustments but before they spillover into the onset of an inflationary spiral as the internal dynamic takes hold. The central authorities within a capitalist economy may also find that there is a need for such temporary measures to be accompanied by some permanent form of prices and incomes policy to deal with the positional inflation created as a result of the positional conflicts between industrial firms and households which are endemic in a capitalist economy.

The problems in formulating and implementing an effective prices and incomes policy may well be nigh impossible to solve. The boundary between normal adjustment and the onset of an inflationary spiral is, at best, narrow and ill-defined. The historical experience of such policies does not augur well. Voluntary agreements by firms and workers have lacked authority. Most centrally enforced policies have been blanket impositions of constraints which have interfered with the normal adjustment process to such an extent that a period of inflation has followed as soon as the restrictions have been lifted. In an attempt to allow the normal adjustment process to take place, many policies have introduced a number of exemptions which have been sufficiently broad as to allow the inflationary spiral to take root. In many cases prices and incomes policies have been wage policies only, dealing with the rate of increase of money wages. Such policies have usually come into conflict with the real-wage objective of workers, since they do not attempt to control prices, the other element in a micro-push inflation. In addition to the question of the fairness in allocating the burden of adjustment to workers, the adoption of wage policies has had two serious consequences. The resulting reduction in the real value of money wages during the period of the policy has meant that the necessary conductive increases in money wages are only deferred until the wage restraints are lifted. Furthermore, wage policies result in a redistribution of income in favour of profits, since industrial firms face no limits on their ability to raise prices. This redistribution of income is likely to have a negative impact on the monetary flow to the extent that the propensity to spend out of profit income is less than the propensity to spend out of wage income. Thus, just as with any employment objective, the central authorities in a capitalist economy face enormous difficulties in achieving a reduction in the rate of inflation using arm's-length methods, difficulties which may be so great as to necessitate more direct methods of social control over the operation of the economy.

7

Towards A Post-Classical Economics: An Agenda

The nature of post-classical economics

Classical theory attempts to provide an understanding of the operation of the capitalist economy by using a single set of presupposed notions of order. Classical theory has developed the theory of an exchange economy in which all economic behaviour is seen to be within the allocative mode of activity. Economic activity is treated as a process of stock adjustment, regulated by the price mechanism within a series of markets. This process is explained by the demand-and-supply theory of price determination, the theoretical core of classical theory. If a market has a perfectly atomistic structure and agents are rational and possess sufficient information, the price mechanism is able to ensure the establishment of the equilibrium outcome of market-clearing. It follows, therefore, that prices and quantities are seen to be determined simultaneously within the same behavioural process. If the price mechanism is able to operate freely and effectively in all markets throughout the economy, this ensures the establishment of a general equilibrium outcome with generalized market-clearing, implying a full-employment level of output. Thus classical theory espouses the doctrine of the invisible hand, the most significant of all its theoretical results. Given the appropriate structural and informational prerequisites, the price mechanism can ensure that all potential gains from trade are exhausted, thus rendering the individual pursuit of self-interest consistent with the achievement of the general welfare of all. If the price mechanism fails to achieve a perfect allocative equilibrium, it follows from classical theory that this is due to the existence of structural and/or informational imperfections which inhibit the operation of market forces. Thus classical theory has developed a number of imperfectionist theories of misallocation to explain the non-attainment of a perfect allocative equilibrium.

The present analysis starts from the fundamental belief that classical theory is insufficient on its own to explain the operation of the capitalist economy. In particular, this analysis has considered the limitations of classical theory with regard to the macro dimension of the capitalist economy. Certain significant forms of economic behaviour do not fall within the allocative mode of activity and hence cannot be correctly understood from the standpoint provided by the classical frame of reference. Thus the limits to the relevance of classical theory must be defined, and alternative, but complementary, frames of reference need to be developed to deal with the non-allocative dimensions of economic activity.

The starting-point for this post-classical theory of the macro economy was provided by Keynes's *General Theory*. Keynes initiated the development of the theory of a monetary production economy to explain the determination of employment in the industrial sector. In a monetary production economy, output and employment are not determined by the price mechanism in an allocative process. In particular, there is no aggregate market for labour in the classical sense of employment and the real wage being determined simultaneously in the manner described by the demand-and-supply theory of price determination. In a monetary production economy, the means of regulation is the multiplier process. The rate of the monetary flow adjusts to ensure that there is no net flow of funds from the monetary flow. This creates the possibility that the monetary flow may be in a dynamic equilibrium which implies insufficient aggregate demand to support a full-employment level of output. Thus a monetary production economy can generate an equilibrium outcome in which there is involuntary unemployment. There is no reason whatsoever for a monetary production economy to move towards a position of full employment.

The post-classical analysis seeks to build on the revolutionary theoretical achievements of Keynes's *General Theory*. The structure of the capitalist economy is such that there are two very different modes of activity at the macro level. The industrial sector and the banking system in the financial sector operate within the utilization mode of activity, and hence it is appropriate to understand behaviour within these parts of the economy using the theory of a monetary production economy. On the other hand, the stock market system in the financial sector operates within the allocative mode of activity and so should be understood using the classical theory of an exchange economy. Thus, post-classical macroeconomics involves a synthesis between classical theory and Keynes's theory of a monetary production economy.

Although the task which is undertaken here is essentially a theoretical one, the motivation is very practical. The scientific pursuit of theoretical order is a purely academic objective which fulfils only the needs of those within the academic community. The pursuit of theoretical order has technological implications. Theories imply the adoption of particular courses of action in order to achieve actual changes. If the theories change, the technological implications may change. It is the technological implications of theories which are the most significant aspect of science for society as a whole. Indeed, many would argue that the technological implications of science should be the most important for the academic community also. Whilst this view can be used to justify quite unacceptable limitations on the academic freedom to pursue theoretical knowledge in whatever direction the scientist wishes, the motivation behind this view is entirely fair. Theoretical scientists cannot claim immunity from the questions of moral responsibility raised by the theories they create. In particular, theoretical economists have a responsibility for the social consequences of the economic policies which they advocate on the basis of their theories. The present analysis is greatly influenced by these moral responsibilities.

The classical doctrine of the invisible hand carries with it the policy prescription that there is no need for systematic intervention in the economic sphere of activity by the central authorities if the price mechanism is able to operate freely and effectively. This policy of *laissez-faire* needs to be supplemented by some limited form of intervention if there are structural and/or informational imperfections which prevent the price mechanism from achieving a perfect allocative equilibrium . In such circumstances there may be some scope for alleviating the macro effects of the failure on the part of the price mechanism through using macroeconomic policies in an attempt to bypass the imperfections which are the ultimate cause of misallocation. The effectiveness of this type of intervention depends crucially on the precise nature of the imperfections which are obstructing the operation of the price mechanism. Thus, in certain special cases, Keynesian demand-management policies may be able to reduce the level of unemployment. In general, however, misallocation requires microeconomic policies designed to remove the structural and/or informational imperfections which are the the ultimate cause of the misallocation.

The post-classical theory of the macro economy gives a very different view of the nature of macroeconomic policy in the capitalist economy. Once it is accepted that the capitalist economy is not an exchange economy in which all economic behaviour is regulated by the price mechanism, it no longer necessarily follows that the *laissez-faire* policy stance is appropriate. The non-allocative behaviour patterns exhibited by individual agents in the capitalist economy create the potential for sub-optimal macro outcomes without any automatic self-correcting mechanisms. Indeed, far from exhibiting any tendency for automatic self-correction, the macro economy may generate cumulative causation processes whereby the adjustment processes initiated by some external shock to the economy, tend to exacerbate the effects of the shock. In the industrial sector, the dependency of the expenditure flow on the monetary flow creates the multiplier process of cumulative causation, while the interaction of the conductive role of prices and wages creates the potential for an inflationary spiral, another form of cumulative causation. In the financial sector, the existence of significant speculative activity creates the potential for cumulative movements in the market prices of traded assets. There is no invisible hand to prevent the macro economy from getting locked into these processes of cumulative causation. The lack of any automatic self-correcting mechanism in significant parts of the macro economy creates a general need for systematic policy intervention by the central authorities in the operation of the capitalist economy, in complete contrast to the *laissez-faire* implications of classical theory.

The post-classical approach to macroeconomic theory provides a justification for Keynesian demand-management policies. This justification comes from assumptions made about the nature of the behaviour patterns which actually exist in the economy. If these assumptions are shown to be generally valid, the policy prescriptions which follow must also be generally valid. This is the proper method of evaluating technological implications of alternative theories. The validation of Keynesian behavioural

assumptions returns Keynesian policy prescriptions to their right-
ful place as the appropriate policy regime for a capitalist economy. This does not mean a return to the naïve hydraulic beliefs of
the early Keynesians. The post-classical analysis presented here is
sceptical of the effectiveness of arm's-length regulation of the
capitalist economy. In particular, the reliance on demand-
management policies to alleviate mass unemployment depends
critically on there being a strong link across the Keynesian Dichotomy which separates the realm of the monetary flow and the
realm of productive activity. The strength of this link is likely to
be at its weakest just at the time when it is required most.
Keynesian policies are a necessary, but by no means a generally
sufficient, condition for the alleviation of mass unemployment in
the capitalist economy. The insufficiency of arm's-length intervention creates the need for more direct forms of social control
of the economic sphere to achieve social objectives. Ultimately
this may mean the creation of a very different form of economy.

The recognition by post-classical theory of the dualistic nature
of the capitalist economy raises the possibility of the capitalist
dilemma facing policy-makers. There is a common interest between households and industrial capital in giving primacy to the
objective of full employment over any inflationary objective in
circumstances in which a choice of objective must be made.
Financial capital, on the other hand, places primacy on the
inflationary objective. This potential for a conflict of interest
between the industrial and financial sectors exists at the level of
choice of means, in addition to the choice of objectives. This
conflict of interest creates an additional dimension to the political
decision over the nature of the macroeconomic policies to be
adopted, a dimension hidden from view for classical theorists by
their blinding acceptance of the doctrine of the invisible hand.

The post-classical analysis of the macro economy has raised,
inevitably, questions about the microeconomic aspects of economic behaviour. The macroeconomic theory presented here is
firmly based on assumptions about the behaviour patterns of
economic agents. Although the present concern has been with the
macro implications of these behaviour patterns, where appropriate, some of the micro implications have been sketched out. In
particular, non-allocative roles of prices and wages have been
outlined with some analysis of the implications with regard to, for
example, the competitive process between firms and wage bar-

gain. The post-classical approach is not limited to the field of macroeconomic theory. There is a need for a post-classical revolution throughout economic theory as a whole. The present analysis is but an imperfect initial contribution to this more general development.

The generality of the post-classical approach follows from the revolutionary change in the method of analysis which it implies. Three particular aspects can be distinguished in the post-classical method of analysis which sets it apart from the classical method of analysis. First, the post-classical approach is a behavioural one. Its starting-point is a series of empirically based assumptions about the behaviour patterns exhibited by agents. The theoretical task is to build models which elucidate the implications of these behaviour patterns. The results of such analyses are only specific to those situations for which the behavioural assumptions are valid. Theoretical economists need to free themselves of the vice of seeking after the holy grail of a general theory, valid for all agents at all times in all places. Classical theorists believe themselves to be in possession of such a theory, namely the theory of rational choice. This belief in the existence of a general theory is a misleading and dangerous myth. The behavioural assumptions implied by the theory of rational choice are obviously non-realistic simplications of many significant contexts of behaviour, yet this criticism is deemed irrelevant through recourse to instrumentalist justifications that it is the predictive power of models which should be the principal criterion for judging theories, irrespective of the realism of the assumptions on which the theories are based. Such instrumentalist arguments represent the ultimate means of rendering any theory immune to all empirically based criticisms of its assumptions. The behavioural approach of post-classical theories denies the validity of the instrumentalist justification for the continued use of non-realistic assumptions. All behavioural assumptions should be tested for their applicability in specific situations. Furthermore, human beings possess the power to think for themselves, changing their subjective evaluations of a particular situation and adjusting their behaviour patterns accordingly. Much to the obvious disappointment of the classical exponents of the theory of rational choice, human beings do not exhibit the properties of continuity over time in their behaviour which is found in the physical world. This has not, of course, prevented classical theory from assuming such continuity to exist and carrying on regardless.

The second important departure in method by the post-classical approach is the explicit recognition of the need to adopt a dynamic method of analysis. The static equilibrium-theoretic approach of classical theory is only applicable to situations in which the equilibrium outcome at any point in time is entirely independent of outcomes in previous periods. Such an analysis is out of time and therefore irrelevant to dynamic processes through time in which the position at any point in time is a reflection of the whole previous historical process of change as well as the current propensities to change. The static equilibrium-theoretic approach is one example of the extreme Procrustean methods to which classical theory tends to resort in pursuit of the definitive objective explanation of economic phenomena. The adoption of a more dynamic method goes hand-in-hand with the realization of the possible bootstraps properties of some economic phenomena. Economic behaviour involves agents striving for a position, possibly non-existent, in which their behaviour patterns are mutually consistent. The particular historical form of the dynamic created by the search for behavioural consistency determines the magnitude of the economic variables involved. Economic variables have the power to pull themselves up by their own historical bootstraps. This bootstraps property is yet another reason why the search for a general theory is ill-conceived. Actual outcomes are dependent on the nature of the particular historical experience from which they have emerged. A general theory cannot overcome the obstacle of historical dependence, despite the best efforts of many classical theorists to sweep this particular problem under the static equilibrium-theoretic carpet.

Finally, the most important departure from classical methods of analysis is the explicit adoption by post-classical theory of a pluralist method. The post-classical approach is founded on the belief that no single frame of reference is necessarily sufficient to provide an adequate understanding of any particular phenomenon. This implies the need to develop alternative but complementary frames of reference to deal with the different aspects of any multi-dimensional whole. The limits to the relevance of each frame of reference must be defined and the interconnections between frames of reference must be explored. In the case of economic theory, the need for such a pluralist approach is created by the existence of non-allocative behaviour. The classical frame of reference interprets all economic behaviour in terms of the allocation-misallocation duality. This highly restrictive presupposition denies the existence of qualitative differences in economic behaviour and, as a consequence, cannot investigate the technological implications of these non-allocative modes of activity. Classical theory is only relevant to the operation of the allocative mode of activity. This is the limit to its relevance. Post-classical theory is a recognition of the need to move beyond the limits of classical theory.

Although many of the arguments expressed are very hostile towards classical theory, and rightly so, the post-classical approach does not mean the rejection of the whole of classical theory – far from it. Classical theory provides a detailed explanation of the allocative mode of activity. The choice-theoretic, market-theoretic and equilibrium-theoretic presuppositions of classical theory may be applicable in particular circumstances. The revolutionary innovation of post-classical theory is the realization of the bounded vision created by interpreting all economic behaviour within the limits imposed by the classical frame of reference. If the proponents of classical theory can accept the existence of such limits to their analysis, this would open the way towards a meaningful and rewarding interaction between classical and non-classical theories. This would also require post-Keynesians to abandon their complete rejection of classical theories. The post-classical approach is founded on the recognition that both classical and post-Keynesian theories are necessary for a fuller understanding of the capitalist economy. Both sets of theories, if reformulated within their respective, clearly defined limits, constitute the components of a truly revolutionary synthesis between classical theory and the ideas contained within Keynes's *General Theory*. Within such a synthesis, classical theory and Keynes's *General Theory* would be seen as complementary frames of reference, rather than irreconcilable alternatives. The classical–Keynesian debate would move on a new plane of theoretical development, characterised by an atmosphere of academic tolerance in which each school of thought recognises the legitimacy and necessity of the other.

An agenda for the future

The present analysis represents a starting-point, a first step on a thousand-mile journey.The analysis indicates one way forward for the study of economics. That way lies in the development of a post-classical economics, a pluralist approach which recognizes the limitations inherent in any particular theory based on a single set of presupposed notions of order. The post-classical approach requires the development of alternative frames of reference, the definition of the limitations to the relevance of each, and the investigation of the interconnections between them. It is this methodological revolution which is the essence of the post-classical approach. The acceptane of the pluralist method is the key objective of the present analysis.

What is offered here is not a general and definitive theory of the capitalist economy. The central concern has been to provide a more general set of presupposed notions of economic order on which to develop a more general theory. The preliminary nature of the present analysis is illustrated by the focus on the question posed by Keynes in *The General Theory*: what is the short-run macro behaviour of a closed capitalist economy? That reflects a recognition of Keynes's path-breaking attempt to understand the nature of orthodox economic theory and develop a more general theory. Keynes's attempt has been the primary influence. However, there is another reason for following Keynes in limiting the focus of attention to the short-run macro behaviour of a closed economy. Such a restricted definition of the object of analysis indicates the provisional nature of the analysis. It is a starting-point suggesting an agenda of future developments required to achieve more detailed theoretical conclusions with more immediate practical relevance than the conclusions drawn here. Too often in the past economists have treated their theories as dogmatic truths beyond question. Such claims to unrivalled authority are dangerous, blinding the proponents of any particular set of beliefs to the possibility of any limitations to their own way of seeing the world. The pluralist method of the post-classical approach precludes dogmatic claims to authority, requiring instead a more critical and pragmatic attitude to all theoretical conclusions. Abstract theory is but an aid to, not a substitute for, understanding the complexity of the real world.

The agenda for future developments suggested here is a long one. At the macro level the analysis must be extended beyond the confines of a closed economy in the short-run. The macro implications of the investment behaviour of firms has been considered only with regard to the short-run effects on the level of aggregate demand. The supply-side implications over the longer run as the capital stock grows must also be reconsidered in the light of the post-classical approach. In a similar vein, the international dimension to the capitalist economy must be brought in. International considerations, for example, may be of primary importance in the determination of the overall level of rates of interest in any single national economy. Furthermore, it is in the international arena that the conflict of interest between industrial and financial capital may be at its most intense. This conflict concerns exchange rate and interest rate policies. For example, industrial capital may prefer a depreciating currency for reasons of export competitiveness, while financial capital may prefer an appreciating currency, in order to attract a greater inflow of foreign capital. Similarly, financial capital may prefer to use increases in domestic rates of interest in order to support the current exchange rate, but such a policy is likely to harm industrial capital through its adverse effects on domestic aggregate demand as well as through its adverse effects on the international competitiveness of domestically produced goods and services. A detailed treatment of these longer-run growth and international considerations is a necessary prerequisite for macro policy prescriptions to be gained from the post-classical approach.

Another important area for future development of the post-classical approach is the theory of the business cycle. Currently the new classical theory of the real business cycle predominates, with the business cycle treated as misallocation in an exchange economy. This new classical approach denies that the monetary context of behaviour plays any significant role. This presupposition must cast severe doubt on the adequacy of real business cycle theory. As yet, however, there is no adequate alternative theory of the business cycle in a monetary production economy. The present analysis of behaviour in a monetary production economy provides the foundations on which such a theory of the monetary business cycle could be built.

As well as extending post-classical macro analysis, much work is required at the micro level. At several points in the present analysis the limitations to the choice-theoretic approach of classical theory have been discussed. The concept of a rational economic agent is of limited usefulness in a world of imperfect information and uncertainty (as opposed to situations of risk). Such a world is characterized by routine behaviour patterns and learning procedures. Mainstream theory has made little headway in developing theories of behaviour under conditions of imperfect information and uncertainty, being content instead with trying to find 'escape routes' back into the world of perfect information and perfect foresight; a comfortable world with the much sought after property of theoretical determinacy. It is to be hoped that more of the economics profession will be prepared to accept eventually these theoretical challenges. In particular, an adequate theory of the formation of expectations and their adaptation is long overdue to counteract the seductive but ultimately dangerously misleading spell cast by the rational-expectations hypothesis.

Another area for future development, at the micro level, is the theory of the competitive process. Classical theory has been concerned with competition as an allocative process, investigating the effects of structural imperfections on that process. Economic theory needs a theory of the competitive process which moves beyond the structuralist approach. This is clearly evident by the continuing failure of classical theory to come to terms with the significance of oligopoly, the most prevalent market condition in modern capitalist economies. Oligopoly is the epitomy of competition in the ordinary, everyday meaning of the term, yet it is patently obvious that the structuralist approach of classical theory is entirely inadequate in explaining the behaviour of oligopolistic firms. Many of those working in the field of industrial economics would accept this, as evidenced by the increasing use of the game-theoretic approach as a more appropriate characterization of the context of behaviour within which oligopolistic firms operate. It is to be hoped that the implications of such non-structuralist theories of competition will come to have a more prominent role in microeconomics as a whole.

It goes almost without saying that the theoretical development of the post-classical approach must go hand-in-hand with its empirical development through application to specific current and historical experience. The theoretical models which are developed must be grounded firmly on empirically based assumptions about actual patterns of behaviour. This is the behavioural method of analysis. A particular theoretical model in economics is relevant only if its assumptions about behaviour are appropriate for the particular situation under analysis. The appropriateness of the assumptions must always be evaluated before claiming any degree of relevancy to a particular economic theory especially if specific policy prescriptions are to be made.

It is not only the limitations to any particular economic theory which must be recognized. The contribution of economic theory as a whole must be seen to be limited. The frames of reference provided by economic theory must be integrated with socio-political, institutional and other non-economic frames of reference drawn from the other disciplines, which are concerned with human behaviour. In this way the post-classical approach can become a stepping-stone towards the development of a more general political economy of capitalism which moves beyond the confines of the frames of reference provided by economic theory. Such a political economy of capitalism would overcome the qualitative fragmentation between disciplines dealing with a common object of analysis, albeit from very different perspectives.

Although the post-classical approach has been developed initially within the field of economic theory, it is not limited to economic theory. The post-classical approach embodies a methodological approach with a much more general application. The post-classical approach advocates the general acceptance of theoretical pluralism in all fields of study. Economics is not alone in being characterized by bounded vision and qualitative fragmentation as a result of the adoption of the traditional methodological stance characterized by a belief in objectivity combined with the presupposition of a reductionist notion of order. The post-classical approach offers a way forward to all fields of study which remain firmly wedded to the traditional methodological stance.

In his *Memoirs of Newton*, Brewster quotes Sir Issac Newton as summing up his work as follows: 'I do not know what I may seem to the world; but to myself I seem to have been only a boy playing on the sea-shore, and diverting myself in now and then finding a smoother pebble or a prettier shell than ordinary, whilst the great ocean of truth lay all undiscovered before me.' We would all do well to remember Newton's humility. This present analysis offers but a small pebble on the shore. A whole ocean, far more extensive than the limited horizons imposed by orthodox belief, lies beyond, waiting to be explored. We must overcome the 'flat earth' mentality, leave behind the security of a well-known coastline and set sail on the voyage of discovery.

Sources and Influences

This appendix provides a guide to the principal sources and influences for the present analysis. Section 1 deals with those sources and influences relating to the particular methodological perspective adopted. Section 2 relates to the three main schools of thought within modern classical macroeconomics with emphasis on the classical Keynesian school, since this classification is peculiar to the present analysis. Finally, section 3 gives some indication of those contributions which can be interpreted as attempts to move beyond the classical frame of reference.

1 Methodology

The traditional falsificationist view of science as the continuous search for empirical refutations of provisionally held hypotheses is associated with Popper (1968). It is this traditional view which is adopted by most economists (see e.g. Stigler 1983). Friedman (1953) adopts this methodological stance in his instrumentalist defence of the use of non-realistic assumptions within economic theory. The falsificationist view has encountered a number of criticisms, the most pertinent being the so-called Duhem–Quine thesis, which calls into question the notion that individual target hypotheses can ever be tested conclusively, since any hypothesis is always tested in conjunction with a whole set of auxiliary hypotheses. Cross (1982) provides a discussion of the Duhem--Quine thesis and its implications for economics. Lakatos (1974) provides a reconstructed falsificationist view of science which recognizes the group nature of scientific theories. Lakatos can be viewed as having provided the conservative response to the implications of the Duhem–Quine thesis and the criticisms of the 'new view' of science.

The 'new view' of science originates with Kuhn (1970). Kuhn sees scientists as operating within scientific communities characterized by their adherence to a single world view or paradigm. Thus Kuhn recognizes that there is what can be seen as a metaphysical dimension to scientific knowledge and, furthermore, that the scientific process cannot be treated as independent of the social, institutional, cultural and historical context in which it takes place. Kuhn's contribution points the way to a more pluralist conception of the nature of science which moves beyond the limits of the traditional perspective. The 'new view' of science emerges from a number of modern writers with perspectives which complement Kuhn's approach. Principal amongst those which have influenced this present analysis are Polanyi (1973), Bohm (1980), Toulmin (1972), Feyerabend (1978), Koestler (1964), Berman (1981) and Capra (1976; 1983). The writings of Berman, Bohm and Capra highlight the dominance of reductionist and mechanistic notions of order in Western thought. Capra, in particular, suggests the bootstrap hypothesis as an alternative to the reductionist approach. This hypothesis is associated with Chew (1968).

Beyond the recent debates in the history and philosophy of science, two other sources have had a significant influence on the methodological stance adopted by this analysis. First, the later philosophy of Wittgenstein (1968), on the context-related nature of language, provides an important and complementary perspective on the nature of science. This application of Wittgenstein's approach is developed by Phillips (1977). Second, Mini (1974) provides a detailed account of the Cartesian foundations of modern economic theory and the continual struggle of some, especially Keynes, to break away.

2 The classical macroeconomics of unemployment

Within modern macroeconomics there are three main schools of thought which share the classical frame of reference: the classical Keynesian school, the neoclassical/monetarist school and the new classical school. The classical Keynesian school have attempted to discover the appropriate classical microfoundations with which to explain Keynesian macro outcomes. The inevitable result has been the elaboration of various imperfectionist theories of misallocation. The classical Keynesian approach began with the ISLM interpretation of Keynes's *General Theory* presented by Hicks (1937). The ISLM interpretation focused only on the demand-side, deriving the equilibrium levels of money income and the rate of interest. In order to derive the associated equilibrium level of employment, Hicks assumed a fixed money-wage. Subsequently, Modigliani (1944) argued that, once the supply side is considered, it is the rigidity of money wages in the labour market which is the ultimate cause of involuntary unemployment in the Keynesian model, except for the special cases when Say's Law breaks down as the result of interest rate maladjustment due to the existence of a liquidity trap or investment being interest-inelastic. This particular interpretation of Keynes's *General Theory* formed the basis of the Neoclassical Synthesis, the first phase in the development of classical Keynesianism.

The second phase began with Patinkin (1965), who argued that the wealth effect, in its direct and indirect forms, would ensure that Say's Law would hold in the long run so that the economy would be in equilibrium at full employment. According to Patinkin, involuntary unemployment is a disequilibrium phenomenon, arising from the slow speeds of price adjustment. This disequilibrium approach was developed further by Clower (1965), Barro and Grossman (1971) and Malinvaud (1977). The disequilibrium approach was set within a Walrasian context by Clower (1965) and Leijonhufvud (1968). This neo-Walrasian approach held that Keynes's disequilibrium analysis dealt with the consequences of false trading at non-market-clearing prices, circumstances which arise theoretically if the assumption of the Walrasian auctioneer is relaxed. Given that the Walrasian auctioneer represents the assumption of perfect information, the writings of the neo-Walrasians, such as Leijonhufvud, pointed the way towards involuntary unemployment being understood as the disequilibrium consequence of slow price adjustment caused by imperfect information. However, the neo-Walrasian analysis never explained why slow price adjustment would result from the behaviour of rational economic agents operating with imperfect information (see Drazen 1980).

The most recent writings in the classical Keynesian approach can be viewed as an attempt to extend the earlier phases of the analysis by providing choice-theoretic analyses of the effects of structural and informational imperfections. Theories of the macro effects of structural imperfections have been developed by, amongst others, Benassy (1976), Grandmont and Laroque (1976), Hart (1982) and Snower (1983). A complementary approach has been developed by Weitzman (1982). In effect, Weitzman has taken one step back from imperfect structure, looking at increasing returns as the ultimate cause of imperfectly competitive market structures. The alternative line of development has been to treat involuntary unemployment as the macro consequence of informational imperfections. This has led to the development of the theory of conjectural equilibrium by Hahn (1978) and Negishi (1979). The theory of conjectural equilibrium shows why rational economic agents with imperfect information may maintain prices at non-market-clearing levels in markets with a perfectly atomistic structure. The theory of conjectural equilibrium builds on the prescient remarks made by Arrow (1959) on the problems of disequilibrium adjustment in perfectly competitive markets. A complementary line of argument to the imperfect information approach has been developed by Howitt (1985). Howitt argues that transactions costs should be treated as the ultimate cause of involuntary unemployment.

The neoclassical/monetarist theories of unemployment have grown out of the demise of the original Phillips curve in the face of the experience of stagflation. The key contribution is that of Friedman (1968). Friedman proposed the expectations-augmented Phillips curve and the associated natural-rate hypothesis. This laid the ground for the emergence of the so-called 'new microeconomics' of unemployment and inflation with particular emphasis on search theories of unemployment (see Phelps 1970). Friedman himself stressed the importance of expectational errors. The new microeconomics focuses on the effects of those types of informational imperfection which lead agents to trade sub-optimal quantities, given the current set of market prices (as opposed to the classical Keynesian theories which deal with those types of informational imperfections which lead agents to maintain prices at non-market-clearing levels). An outgrowth of the new microeconomics has been the new classical approach (see e.g. Lucas and Sargent 1981). The new classical approach is characterized by the twin propositions of market-clearing and the rational expectations hypothesis. That hypothesis was first proposed by Muth (1961).

3   Beyond classical theory

The principal catalyst to the development of the present analysis has been the writings of Keynes. The most influential elements in Keynes's thought have been *The General Theory of Employment, Interest and Money* (VII), the *Treatise on Probability* (VIII), the essay entitled 'My Early Beliefs' (X, pp. 433–51), and the various papers written while *The General Theory* was being developed and after its publication (XIII, XIV and XXIX), especially the so-called *QJE* 1937 article (XIV, pp. 109–23) as well as the writings on the monetary production economy (XXIX, pp. 49–102). Incidentally, it was Keynes's writings on the monetary production economy which suggested the stylistic approach of comparing three different economies which is used here, although the classification used differs, in quite significant ways, from Keynes's own classification.

The interpretations placed herein on Keynes's work have been largely derived from many of the contributions of the post-Keynesian school. Harcourt (1982) provides an excellent survey of the diverse strands of thought within the post-Keynesian school. Particularly important have been the writings of the 'fundamentalist Keynesians', a designation used by Coddington (1976). Prominent in this group have been Robinson (1964, 1974) and Shackle (1967).

Another strand of thought, within the post-Keynesian school, is the neo-Ricardian approach associated with writings of Eatwell (1979) and Milgate (1982). The neo-Ricardian influence on the present analysis has been an entirely negative one. The neo-Ricardians have attempted to produce a synthesis between Keynes's principle of effective demand and the early classical theories of value and distribution as reformulated by Sraffa (1960). Such an interpretation is clearly at odds with Keynes's unequivocal statement that he sought to break away from both the early classical and the later neoclassical approaches which he considered to share a common set of presuppositions. The neo-Ricardians are strong in their logical critique of the problems which neoclassical theory encounters in its use of the concept of aggregate capital, but the alternative they propose does an injustice to the writings of both Sraffa and Keynes. The neo-Ricardians have gone off on the completely wrong track, ignoring or dismissing much of Keynes's concern with the implications of the dynamic and uncertain context of behaviour in the capitalist economy.

Another influence has been the writings of Kalecki (1939, 1971). Kalecki's writings have, quite rightly, received increasing attention in recent years, particularly by the post-Keynesian school (see e.g. Sawyer 1982). Kalecki has influenced much of the writings of the monopoly capitalism approach (see Cowling 1982). Kalecki explicitly based his analysis on the non-orthodox microfoundations of mark-up pricing, with the size of the mark-up being determined by the degree of monopoly (see Kriesler 1987).

The behavioural approach adopted here by the present analysis has drawn heavily on the writings of Simon (1959, 1976). The approach has been applied in the theory of the firm by Cyert and March (1963). For myself, the possibilities created by the behavioural approach were suggested by Allison (1971). The methodological importance to classical theory of the choice-theoretic approach is discussed by Latsis (1976).

At the micro level, my arguments have drawn heavily on the work of a number of writers who have attempted to move beyond the classical treatment of the competitive process. An important survey of the limitations to the classical approach is provided by McNulty (1968). The starting-point for the critique of the classical approach is the seminal contribution of Sraffa (1926). Sraffa provided a detailed and devastating critique of both the logic and the empirical relevance of the theory of perfect competition. The major break from the classical approach was made by Chamberlin (1933). Chamberlin gave an alternative conception of the competitive process which recognizes the significance of product differentiation as a crucial characteristic of the context of behaviour of firms. A similar approach was adopted by Mason (1939). The limitations of the classical approach became most apparent in the field of oligopoly theory. Rothschild's article (1947) remains one of the most perceptive analyses of oligopoly, which advocates the need to view competition as a process of strategic interaction. The principles of strategic behaviour are detailed by Schelling (1980). The need to adopt a dynamic method of analysis in order to understand oligopolistic behaviour was recognized by Sweezy (1939). Sweezy presented the kinked demand curve analysis in which he shows that the expectations which firms hold about their rivals' reaction patterns are such as to lead to price rigidity even in the face of changes in demand and cost conditions.

In addition, there have been moves beyond the classical approach at the micro level with regards to the analysis of the labour market. The segmented labour market approach denies the existence of auction-type labour markets in many areas of the economy. Instead, employer–employee relationships are seen as forming what are called internal labour markets in which auction-determined bargains are replaced by behaviour based on rules and customs. Okun (1981) characterizes the move from auction-type to custom-type markets as the replacement of the invisible hand by the invisible handshake. The segmented labour-market approach has been developed by, amongst others, Kerr (1954), Doeringer and Piore (1971), Gordon (1972) and Rubery (1978).

Another general influence has stemmed from some of the contributions of those within the Marxist mode of analysis. There is much in the writings of Marx to support the claim that he was the first major post-classical economist. However, this present analysis owes little directly to Marx. However, from within the Marxist political economy tradition, the writings of Rowthorn (1980, 1981) have been an important source of inspiration.

Finally, there have been numerous general critiques of orthodox economic theory which have inspired my search for a more adequate alternative. The most influential of these are those of Leontief (1971), Phelps Brown (1972), Worswick (1972), Hutchison (1977), Balogh (1982) and Steindl (1984).

References

Allison, G. T. 1971: *Essence of Decision*. Boston: Little, Brown & Co.

Arrow, K. J. 1959: Toward a theory of price adjustment. In M. Abramovitz et al., *The Allocation of Economic Resources*. Stanford: Stanford University Press.

Balogh, T. 1982: *The Irrelevance of Conventional Economics*. London: Weidenfield & Nicolson.

Barro, R. J. and Grossman, H. I. 1971: A general disequilibrium model of income and employment. *American Economic Review*, 61, 82–93.

Benassy, J. P. 1976: The disequilibrium approach to monopolistic price setting and general monopolistic equilibrium. *Review of Economic Studies*, 43, 69–81.

Berman, M. 1981: *The Re-enchantment of the World*. Ithaca/London: Cornell University Press.

Bohm, D. 1980: *Wholeness and the Implicate Order*. London: Routledge & Kegan Paul.

Capra, F. 1976: *The Tao of Physics*. London: Fontana.

Capra, F. 1983: *The Turning Point*. London: Fontana.

Chamberlin, E. H. 1933: *The Theory of Monopolistic Competition*. Cambridge, Mass.: Harvard University Press.

Chew, G. 1968: 'Bootstrap': a scientific idea. *Science*, 161, 762–5.

Clower, R. W. 1965: The Keynesian counter-revolution: a theoretical appraisal. In F. H. Hahn, and R. Brechling (eds.), *The Theory of Interest Rates*, London: Macmillan.

Coddington, A. 1976: Keynesian economics: the search for first principles. *Journal of Economic Literature*, 14, 1258–73.

Cowling, K. 1982: *Monopoly Capitalism*. London: Macmillan.

Cross, R. 1982: The Duhem–Quine thesis, Lakatos, and the appraisal of theories in macroeconomics. *Economic Journal*, 92, 320–40.

Cyert, R. M. and March, J. G. 1963: *A Behavioural Theory of the Firm*. Englewood Cliffs, N J: Prentice-Hall.

Doeringer, P. and Piore, M. 1971: *Internal Labor Markets and Manpower Analysis*. Lexington, Mass.: D. C. Heath & Co.

Drazen, A. 1980: Recent developments in macroeconomic disequilibrium theory. *Econometrica*, 48, 283–306.

Eatwell, J. 1979: *Theories of Value and Output, and Employment.* London: Thames Papers in Political Economy.

Feyerabend, P. 1978: *Against Method.* London: Verso.

Friedman, M. 1953: The methodology of positive economics. In *Essays in Positive Economics*, Chicago: University of Chicago Press.

Friedman, M. 1968: The role of monetary policy. *American Economic Review*, 58, 1–17.

Gordon, D. M. 1972: *Theories of Poverty and Underemployment.* Lexington, Mass.: D. C. Heath & Co.

Grandmont, J. M. and Laroque, G. 1976: On temporary Keynesian equilibria. *Review of Economic Studies*, 43, 69–81.

Hahn, F. H. 1978: On non-Walrasian equilibria. *Review of Economic Studies*, 45, 1–17.

Harcourt, G. C. 1982: *Post-Keynesianism: Quite Wrong and/or Nothing New?* London: Thames Papers in Political Economy.

Hart, O. 1982: 'A model of imperfect competition with Keynesian features. *Quarterly Journal of Economics*, 96, 109–38.

Hicks, J. R. 1937: Mr Keynes and the 'Classics': a suggested interpretation. *Econometrica*, 5, 147–59.

Howitt, P. 1985: Transactions costs and unemployment. *American Economic Review*, 75, 88–100.

Hutchison, T. W. 1977: *Knowledge and Ignorance in Economics.* Oxford: Basil Blackwell.

Kalecki, M. 1939: *Essays in the Theory of Economic Fluctuations.* London: Allen & Unwin.

Kalecki, M. 1971: *Dynamics of the Capitalist Economy.* Cambridge: Cambridge University Press.

Kerr, C. 1954: The Balkanisation of labour markets: In E. W. Bakke and P. M. Hauser (eds), *Labor Mobility and Economic Opportunity*, Cambridge, Mass.: MIT Press.

Keynes, J. M. 1973–81: *The Collected Writings of John Maynard Keynes*, vols I–XXIX. Edited for the Royal Economic Society by E. Johnson, D. Moggridge and Sir A. Robinson, London/Cambridge: Macmillan/Cambridge University Press
(VII) *The General Theory of Employment, Interest and Money.*
(VIII) *Treatise on Probability.*
(X)   *Essays in Biography.*
(XIII) *The General Theory and After. Part I: Preparation.*
(XIV) *The General Theory and After. Part II: Defence and Development.*
(XXIX) *The General Theory and After (Supplement to Volumes XIII and XIV).*

Koestler, A. 1964: *The Act of Creation.* London: Hutchinson.

Kriesler, P. 1987: *Kalecki's Microanalysis.* Cambridge: Cambridge University Press.

Kuhn, T. S. 1970: *The Structure of Scientific Revolutions*, 2nd edn Chicago: University of Chicago Press.

Lakatos, I. 1974: Falsification and the methodology of scientific research programmes. In I. Lakatos and A. Musgrave (eds), *Criticism and the Growth of Knowledge*, Cambridge: Cambridge University Press.

Latsis, S. J. 1976: A research programme in economics. In S. J. Latsis (ed.), *Method and Appraisal in Economics*, Cambridge: Cambridge University Press.

Leijonhufvud, A. 1968: *On Keynesian Economics and the Economics of Keynes*. Oxford: Oxford University Press.

Leontief, W. 1971: Theoretical assumptions and nonobserved facts. *American Economic Review*, 61, 1–7.

Lucas, R. E. and Sargent, T. J. S. 1981: *Rational Expectations and Econometric Practice*. London: Allen & Unwin.

McNulty, P. 1968: Economic theory and the meaning of competition. *Quarterly Journal of Economics*, 82, 1–33.

Malinvaud, E. 1977: *The Theory of Unemployment Reconsidered*. Oxford: Basil Blackwell.

Mason, E. S. 1939: Price and production policies of large-scale enterprise. *American Economic Review (Suppl.)*, 29, 61–74.

Milgate, M. 1982: *Capital and Employment*. London: Academic Press.

Mini, P. 1974: *Philosophy and Economics*. Gainesville, Fla.: University of Florida Press.

Modigliani, F. 1944: Liquidity preference and the theory of interest and money. *Econometrica*, 12, 45–88.

Muth, J. F. 1961: Rational expectations and the theory of price movements. *Econometrica*, 29, 315–35.

Negishi, T. 1979: *Microeconomic Foundations of Keynesian Macroeconomics*. Amsterdam: North Holland.

Okun, A. 1981: *Prices and Quantities*. Oxford: Basil Blackwell.

Patinkin, D. 1965: *Money, Interest and Prices*, 2nd ed. New York: Harper & Row.

Phelps, E. S. (ed.) 1970: *Microeconomic Foundations of Employment and Inflation Theory*. New York: W. W. Norton & Co.

Phelps Brown, E. H. 1972: The underdevelopment of economics. *Economic Journal*, 82, 1–10.

Phillips, D. L. 1977: *Wittgenstein and Scientific Knowledge*, London: Macmillan.

Polanyi, M. 1973: *Personal Knowledge*. London: Routledge & Kegan Paul.

Popper, K. R. 1968: *The Logic of Scientific Discovery*. London: Hutchinson.

Robinson, J. 1964: *Economic Philosophy*. Harmondsworth: Penguin.

Robinson, J. 1974: *History versus Equilibrium*. London: Thames Papers in Political Economy.

Rothschild, K. W. 1947: Price theory and oligopoly. *Economic Journal*, 57, 299–320.

Rowthorn, B. 1980: *Capitalism, Conflict and Inflation*, London: Lawrence & Wishart.

Rowthorn, B. 1981: *Demand, Real Wages and Economic Growth*. London: Thames Papers in Political Economy.

Rubery, J. 1978: Structured labour markets, worker organisation, and low pay. *Cambridge Journal of Economics*, 2, 17–36.

Sawyer, M. C. 1982: *Macro-economics in Question*. Brighton: Wheatsheaf.

Schelling, T. C. 1980: *The Strategy of Conflict*. Harvard/London: Harvard University Press.

Shackle, G. L. S. 1967: *The Years of High Theory*. Cambridge: Cambridge University Press.

Simon, H. A. 1959: Theories of decision-making in economics and behavioural science. *American Economic Review*, 49, 253–83.

Simon, H. A. 1976: From substantive to procedural rationality. In S. J. Latsis (ed.), *Method and Appraisal in Economics*, Cambridge: Cambridge University Press.

Snower, D. J. 1983: Imperfect competition, unemployment and crowding-out. *Oxford Economic Papers*, 35, 245–70.

Sraffa, P. 1926: The laws of return under competitive conditions. *Economic Journal*, 36, 535–50.

Sraffa, P. 1960: *Production of Commodities by Means of Commodities*. Cambridge: Cambridge University Press.

Steindl, J. 1984: Reflections on the present state of economics. *Banca Nazionale del Lavoro*, 148, 3–14.

Stigler, G. J. 1983: Nobel Lecture: The process and progress of economics. *Journal of Political Economy*, 91, 529–45.

Sweezy, P. 1939: Demand under conditions of oligopoly. *Journal of Political Economy*, 47, 568–73.

Toulmin, S. 1972: *Human Understanding, Vol. 1*. Oxford: Clarendon Press.

Weitzman, M. L. 1982: Increasing returns and the foundations of unemployment theory. *Economic Journal*, 92, 787–804.

Wittgenstein, L. 1968: *Philosophical Investigations*, 3rd ed. Oxford: Basil Blackwell.

Worswick, G. D. N. 1972: Is progress in economics science possible? *Economic Journal*, 82, 73–86.

Index